Behind the Chinese Miracle

Migrant Workers Tell Their Stories

Lü Guoguang

LONG RIVER PRESS

Published in association with Foreign Languages Press Co. Ltd
24 Baiwanzhuang Road, Beijing 100037, China

ISBN 978-1-59265-099-6

Published in the United States of America by
Sinomedia International Group
Long River Press
360 Swift Ave., Suite 48
South San Francisco, CA 94080

Editors: Liu Fangnian, Chris Robyn

Library of Congress Cataloging-in-Publication Data

Lü, Guoguang.
Behind the Chinese miracle : migrant workers tell their stories / Lü Guoguang.
p. cm.
ISBN 978-1-59265-099-6 (pbk.)
1. Migrant labor--China--Case studies. 2. Agricultural laborers--Employment--China--Case
studies. 3. Rural-urban migration--Social aspects--China--Case studies. I. Title.
HD5856.C5L82 2012
331.6'20951--dc23
                                      2011048181

Printed in China
First Edition

Foreword

Around the turn of the 21st century, the mobility of farmers, one of the key factors influencing Chinese society, made an immense contribution to China's development in three ways. First, rural migrant workers contributed tremendously to the sustained, rapid economic growth of China following the adoption of the reform and opening-up policy in 1978. Second, the mobility of farmers reinforced social stability. According to American political scientist Samuel P. Huntington, farmers exert a profound influence on social stability and turbulence in developing countries. The urbanization process and the consequent opportunities for mobility gave an enormous surplus rural work force a viable alternative to farming. Third, the mobility of farmers fostered institutional innovation by breaking down the urban-rural divide, facilitating the interflow of production factors between the cities and the countryside, and driving economic integration. From the 1990s, Chinese farmers had started doing temporary work in the cities during slack periods in the farming calendar to supplement their family incomes. The flows of rural products and labor forces into the cities, and urban merchandise and information into the countryside, boosted urban-rural economic exchanges and facilitated the transformation of the self-sufficient small farm economy.

Significant historical social progress is often related to the toils and struggles of individuals. The mobility of Chinese farmers has extremely complicated social roots.

Since the adoption of the reform and opening-up policy in 1978, the most noticeable change to Chinese farmers is that they have become involved in an open social system and their work, lifestyle and relationships have become increasingly socialized. In an era of rapid socialization, financial status is a major driver of the social connections of an individual and his/her family, as well as a source of pressure.

Therefore, for farmers who leave their land and hometown, working in the cities offers not only inevitable hardships, but also the excitement of exploring a new way of life. Their lives are busy and hard, and they experience a set of conflicting emotions. Over a hundred million rural migrant workers form a society with high population mobility.

This book presents a vivid picture of the excitement and curiosity of the rural migrant workers, and the benefits that have accrued to them after venturing forth from their villages, as well as the hardships, pain, and bewilderment they have endured after making their way to the cities. From the book we can learn about the real lives, thoughts, and feelings of individuals who make up this group of people. Impelled to quit their familiar homelands for a variety of reasons, they find themselves in a strange new world and make their new lives with their own hands. Many of them have gained rewards that would never have been available to them from the land. Now, more and more rural migrant workers are taking planes to return home for the Spring Festival. We realize that the world really is changing. But it should be borne in mind that in spite of these rewards, their lives are full of hardship and struggle. Suffering from a want of knowledge and skills, and lacking certain institutional privileges, rural migrant workers have to struggle hard against fate, discrimination, and rejection. It is apparent that the mobile population is becoming a marginalized group at the bottom of the social hierarchy. However, without this group society would immediately lose vigor, and stability would be at risk.

The large population of rural migrant workers has become a prominent phenomenon in Chinese society, and has created a unique group and lifestyle. Along with society, the group itself is experiencing significant changes. For example, "rural migrant worker" is no longer an accurate term for describing those born in the 1980s. Most of the 80s-generation migrant workers have never cultivated the land, setting out to find jobs in the cities after dropping out of school. They possess no farming skills, neither do they have much urban experience. This is an unstable, emergent group that deserves attention. Many of the narrators in this book belong to this 80s-generation. Their narratives expose to us a new and diversified world.

In a sense, the rural migrant workers are an integral part of the nation's development, of our life and of the future. From a historical point of view, the term "rural migrant worker" will in due course become a thing of the past. What we are witnessing today will become history. The narratives of rural migrant workers will be part of that history. The narrators and compilers of this book should be commended for recording this history.

Xu Yong, Central China Normal University

Contents

Preface

Over the past few decades, the subject of "rural migrant workers" has been a focus of attention for the academic community, government decision-making departments, and the media. Material about rural migrant workers makes frequent appearances in many fields, including literature, sociology, politics, economics and education. Elites from various fields have cast their eye over the rural migrant worker group as they have come to appreciate the group's important role in remolding the structure and order of society during the ongoing process of social transformation and urbanization.

The absence of a common guarantee system protecting the rights and interests of rural migrant workers has attracted widespread attention from the mass media and the general public. Academic research regarding rural migrant workers concentrates on two aspects: one is policy research based on the composition and character of rural migrant worker groups, and their impact on their hometowns and the cities where they work; the other is quantitative research on the impact of industrialization and urbanization on social transformation and institutional innovation related to the rural-urban divide, the household registration system, and labor-capital relations, and research on the living conditions and development of rural migrant workers. It is noticeable that relevant academic research tends to analyze the conditions and problems of rural migrant workers mostly from the point of view of an administrator or an "urban resident." Records documenting the activities and thoughts of rural migrant workers themselves are rarely seen.

Academic research that respects the history of the lower strata places an emphasis on fieldwork, a common practice of sociology, ethnology and anthropology, and collects oral accounts through direct surveys and interviews with the people concerned. This is of great theoretical value and practical significance in contemporary society. The voices of those rural migrant workers who are struggling at the bottom of society and mostly incapable of writing for publication will effectively be silenced if no one listens to and records them. In that case, the true experiences of them may fade from history.

So I consider that it is not only necessary and but also absolutely imperative to conduct comprehensive research on the education, life, and work experiences of rural migrant workers, and to tell their stories in their own words rather than in the third person. In this way, such research can provide supplements and evidence to history as well as revise or even change people's misconceptions.

Additionally, the implementation of such research was motivated by my personal experience.

During the Spring Festival of 1993, a friend's account of the deception that led to him becoming a "laborer" in Shanxi left a deep impression on me. After the conversation, I began looking for the opportunity of conducting deeper research into the rural migrant worker group and publishing a book offering a comprehensive and objective account of the group's education and work experiences. I believed that their educational background had an impact bearing on their living conditions in their later years.

A decade later, during a survey of children dropping out of school in central and western rural areas of China, I heard many stories about these children leaving their homes to work in the cities. The idea that I had pursued 10 years previously returned to me. My partners and I devised the analysis tools just before the winter vacation of 2006 and started recruiting and training participants. After thorough discussions, we chose "an oral history of the education and life of rural migrant workers" as the subject of our research and defined the stylistic rules and layout.

During our research, we conducted face-to-face sessions with rural migrant workers and heard many stories, both sad and happy. Some of them were still very young and worked with the aim of helping their brothers and sisters attend school, or of paying for the medical expenses of their families, things that seem to come so easily to urban people of their age. They assume responsibility for their families, for their friends and for their loved ones.

The individual stories presented in this book were collected from the rural areas of Hebei, Hubei, Hunan, Anhui, Zhejiang, Fujian and Guangxi during a month's fieldwork conducted around the turn of the year 2006. The researchers carried out the survey as undergraduates gaining experience in the practice of social work. The researchers' notes and the narratives of nearly 200 rural migrant workers are the primary sources of the book. The survey used a targeted sampling of rural households which could provide maximum information relevant to the subject of research. The survey instruments included questionnaires and interview outlines. The questionnaires were aimed at collecting basic information from the interviewees. Those with rich life experiences, and a strong ability to reflect on those experiences and to express themselves, were then listed as key targets for follow-up research. The interview outlines were intended to provide a comprehensive understanding of rural migrant workers through objective, in-depth, and detailed depictions of all aspects of their life, including their educational background and their work experience in the cities.

Before each interview, we asked the interviewee for permission to record the conversation. In cases where we did not receive this permission we would take handwritten notes. We also collected items such as homework assignments and reward and punishment records left from their school days, as well as train tickets for travels between the cities and their hometowns, personal income and expenses accounts, and photos of their life in the cities. Such objects embody their mindset and culture, and add wealth to our case studies.

Our research findings are presented in written form. Our case study write-ups follow four principles that are commonly adopted in oral history research. First, truthfully presenting the viewpoints of people being studied; second, explaining the methods used by the researchers and their relevant reflection during the research; third, depicting the circumstances of the conversations, and the reactions, expression and gestures of people being studied; fourth, probing deeper into individual cases within the broader context of society, culture and economy.

During our research, we received support from the members of the Education Research Group of Huanggang Normal University, Hubei. I would like to extend my sincere gratitude to Professors Cheng Jingbao, Li Jinqi, Zheng Zhongmei and Yuan Xiaopeng of the university's School of Education Science and Technology, who took an active interest in the progress of our survey and the documentation of our research results, and provided detailed guidance and valuable help.

I would also like to express thanks to "Cheung Kong Scholar"

Prof Xu Yong of Central China Normal University for his encouragement and appreciation. His foreword adds weight to this book.

The publication of this book involved the collaborative efforts of many people. Those who conducted the interviews, sorted the audio recordings and wrote the narratives include Ye Haihong, Shang Mengying, Huang Yanting, Yuan Guifeng, Zhang Ting, Yue Jun, Liu Honghong, Qin Meng, Wei Juhua, Chai Xiaoqin, Wang Wensi, Ma Lijun, Liu Yao, Wang Changxing, Chen Pengfei, Yang Xue, Yan Qiaoli, Feng Huiling, Wang Jingjing and Zhang Qiaoling. In addition to conducting interviews and writing the narratives, Zhang Chunping and Li Zhuang helped me edit the writings and carried out a great deal of organization and coordination work.

It should be noted that confusion about dates, individuals and relationships was inevitable when interviewees were recalling early memories. Moreover, when they reviewed the past from a current perspective, it was like viewing distant scenery through colored glasses. Since oral narration is greatly influenced by factors such as time and place and the target of the conversation, the narrative may vary under different circumstances. Memory loss and bias are significant factors affecting oral narratives. In spite of our best efforts to rectify erroneous statements by a variety of means, errors and mistakes are inevitable in the book due to the nature of oral narration. Readers are welcome to identify and comment on any such mistakes.

A Family of Rural Migrant Workers

Narrator 1: Old Du, male, 53, from Ducheng Town of Huanggang City, Hubei Province
Job: bamboo chopstick maker
Work place: Guiyang, Guizhou Province

Narrator 2: Du Jianguo, male, 22, first child of Old Du
Job: hair salon assistant
Work place: Wenzhou, Zhejiang Province

Narrator 3: Du Jianhong, female, 19, adopted child of Old Du
Job: shoe factory worker
Work place: Wenzhou, Zhejiang Province

Old Du: One of the First Rural Migrant Workers in the 1980s

I Was One of the First Rural Migrant Workers

I'm Old Du, 53 years old. As the popular expression goes, I was the first in my home village to "taste the crab." After the Spring Festival in 1988, I took my seven-month pregnant wife and our three-year-old boy Jianguo to Guizhou Province by train and set out to seek our fortune there.

At that time China's railway transportation capacity was limited, and train tickets were in short supply. I turned to a relative in Guiyang for help and finally get two tickets from Wuchang in Hubei to Guiyang in Guizhou. It was the first time that our family had traveled so far. All of us were excited, and at the same time a bit anxious. Actually, I was very nervous.

If my wife were to go into labor on the train, the conditions were far from satisfactory and my wife and the baby would have been in danger. Most of the passengers were neatly dressed and on their way to visit relatives and friends. I stood out in my threadbare military-style coat. The term "rural migrant worker" had not yet been coined. Few farmers had the courage to seek jobs in the cities. In addition, our tickets were for standing room only, so we had to sit on the floor of the aisle all through the journey. I felt nervous and uneasy all the way, and feared I might be targeted by thieves. Before we left home, I bound all our money, a total of 300 yuan, around my calves. As a result, by the time we got off the train the banknotes were well and truly crumpled.

After three nights and two days of bumping and banging, we finally arrived in Guiyang. My three-year-old boy cried ceaselessly in the bamboo basket on my back. Due to our train's late arrival, my relative did not show up at the train station. Perhaps all this foretold that our urban life would not be plain sailing. My pregnant wife and I took our luggage and set off on foot, asking directions along the way. We finally found ourselves at the address that my relative had given us in a letter.

We were disappointed by the absence of the bustling and wealthy scenes that we had expected. My fellow villagers who had been to coastal cities like Guangzhou had provided us with fabulous accounts of these cities. In contrast, what we saw in Guiyang was only a few high-rises that lined the narrow streets. In my bewilderment I began to regret the decision to bring my family to this strange city in the hope of making our fortune. Unaccustomed to the local climate and the constant high temperature, my wife and our boy began to lose weight. I worried about how we could make a living in the city.

Temporary Residence Permit

Guizhou was an agricultural province, and my relatives living there were ordinary workers. There was as yet no structured recruitment system in place. For some considerable time after our arrival I struggled to find a proper job. Unlike the countryside, all the basic needs of daily life, including food, clothes, accommodation and transport, had to be paid for. I came under all sorts of pressures.

After graduating from senior high school, I spent a couple of years learning carpentry and masonry. For the first few years after our marriage I had been a tofu vendor. In the countryside I was considered quite a capable fellow. After a first period of frustration and depression in the city, I tried to take stock and work out how to make a living and support my family. With the help of my relative's family, I found work as a construction laborer. There were few "rural migrant workers" on the construction sites at the time. I did not find the work particularly hard. My first month's salary was 53.8 yuan, a big sum of money for a farmer, who was accustomed to being at the mercy of land and weather.

I was satisfied with the situation, and had decided to continue in construction work, when residence registration became a major problem for the family. During my second month as a construction laborer, police officers came to the construction site to check on workers from outside the city of Guiyang. The state exercised rather strict control on the mobile population. Farmers had to meet certain requirements and go through the relevant procedures before they could work in the cities. I found myself classified in the mobile population and fined, and was almost sent back to my hometown.

The delivery of our second child should have been a happy event, but it resulted in further trouble for us. Giving birth to a baby in the city was hard if a person didn't have a temporary residence permit. Since we did not have one, no hospital would admit my wife, and our baby girl would not be eligible for registration after her birth. To add to our misfortunes, I was fired. But with the help of my relative's family and a midwife, my wife successfully delivered our baby girl Weihua.

More than three months had flown by since our arrival in the city. I used to say during those days that I missed the country life.

After Weihua's birth and my wife's one-month recovery period, our family left my relative's home and moved into a basement of less than 20 square meters in a Guiyang suburb. The night sky here was very beautiful, with as many stars as my hometown. But I was not in a position to appreciate the spectacle. I missed my hometown house of clay and bricks, shabby yet warm; I missed my aged parents and my small plot of land. But I said to myself, "What will my fellows think of me if I go back like this? How can I give my kids a good life if I give up so easily on my dream of making my fortune?" I had to find a way out of my plight.

People in penury will want to change their life, and their life will be better if they make the effort to change. I brushed up my carpentry skills, and as a result we were able to obtain our temporary residence permits. But only two members of the family could stay in the city.

My wife and I talked it over and decided that our daughter and I would stay in Guiyang. My wife returned to our hometown with our son. I trusted our little girl to the care of my relative in Guiyang while I went to a small town in northwest Guizhou to work as a "rural migrant worker" making chopsticks.

My Own Factory

In 1992, tourism in Guizhou was starting to prosper and the chopstick trade was booming. At the end that year, as I expected to collect a handsome salary and celebrate a happy new year with my family in Hubei, I suffered a heavy blow. Just a couple of days before the Spring Festival, our heartless boss fled with all our money leaving all the workers waiting for their salaries.

The chopstick factory had been transferred to the fugitive by our previous boss, a man whom we truly trusted. Having no understanding of the law, we had not signed any contract with our new boss. The previous boss certainly would not take responsibility for the problem, and the new boss was nowhere to be found. Six months of work had gone to waste.

By then I had spent four lonely years in Guizhou and homesickness finally overcame my desire to earn money. That year I rejoined my family in our hometown and we enjoyed a peaceful Spring Festival together.

Tragically, before the end of Spring Festival my relative in Guiyang called to say our daughter Weihua had been missing for three days and had probably been abducted by traffickers. We were stricken by the news. Our smiles immediately turned to tears of grief. After making arrangements for our son, my wife and I set out to look for our daughter.

Heaven seemed to have no pity for our poor and ill-fated family. We spent two months searching around Guiyang and neighboring provinces and cities, but found no trace of Weihua. Under the pressures of daily life, we had to give up our search. Carrying both mental and financial burdens, I began a new stage in my career.

After several years of laboring I had managed to put together some savings. I talked things over with my parents, and they contributed all their savings too. With this, I decided to become my own boss. Having been a chopstick maker, I had some contacts with clients and suppliers. So I started my own business – a small chopstick factory. Issues regarding capital, raw materials and workshop location were solved relatively smoothly. My wife and I were determined to do everything we could to develop our own business.

The workshop was located in our basement in the suburb of Guiyang. A few axes and a small chopstick machine were all our "fixed assets." The texture of bamboo requires special manufacturing techniques. I had invested in only rudimentary equipment, so our production process involved converting the raw material into crude sticks, and then polishing the burrs of the sticks by hand. As a result, our profit was low – we earned less than 1 *jiao* (=0.1 yuan) from each pair of chopsticks. But I was still contented because I was providing for myself and my family with my own hands. I felt I could be considered a proper urban resident.

Our factory developed steadily and our life was improving. To increase our profits, my wife and I got up at 5 in the morning and worked until 11 or even later at night. Hand-polished chopsticks were of better quality, but our hands were often pierced and bleeding from the bamboo splinters. I traveled from one chopstick market to another to expand my business. I had been to almost all the bamboo chopstick markets in Guiyang, big and small. I had encountered frosty receptions and experienced the joy of successful deals. The hardships of business taught me the importance of knowledge.

For a farmer like me without any special training, the market was the key to more business connections. But there were also risks to be taken. My workshop produced chopsticks from good raw materials, and my chopsticks sold well. Through my former laboring experience and in the light of current developments, I realize that even though we perform physical labor, rural workers should master at least one skill and have some basic legal and business knowledge.

Returning Home

18 years passed from 1988 to 2006, and a father became a grandfather. But as I advance in years, my dream of making my fortune remains just that – a dream. This year I returned to my hometown and resumed the simple lifestyle of laboring in the fields from sunrise to sunset. When I was young, I always dreamed of using clean tap water and watching TV programs like urban residents did. Now the countryside has all these things. I tried to leave the countryside and finally I have found myself returning. I will spend the rest of my life laboring and sweating on the land.

Du Jianguo: a Second-generation Rural Migrant Worker

A Young "Farmer" Who Doesn't Know How to Farm

I'm Old Du's son, 22 years old. My parents spent many years working in the cities, so I was left at home most of the time and brought up by my grandparents. Due to a lack of parental discipline and my own nature, I didn't have much interest in studying at school. After graduating from senior high school, I followed my parents' "orders" and joined the army. Two years of army life cured me of plenty of bad habits. In addition, I learned hairdressing, which now earns me a living.

According to what I see in the newspapers, people of my age are called the "80s generation." But I'm not "selfish, spoiled or spendthrift," terms that are often used to describe the 80s generation. I think ignorance of farming and crops is the most obvious characteristic that urban young people like me share in common. I can't even do basic farm work like weeding, fertilizing and rice transplanting. I don't have the mental attachment to the land of my parents.

Working in a Hair Salon

After I left the army, a fellow soldier introduced me to a hair salon in coastal Wenzhou, Zhejiang Province. In spite of my good skills, I did not have the necessary qualification certificates. The hair salon applied strict rules. I had to start as an apprentice. My daily work was washing faces, massaging heads, and drying the customers' hair. Such work appeared to be easy and simple, yet required a good attitude to service, and some skill. Every day I worked right through from 8 in the morning to 12 at night. My hands turned pale and the skin on my fingers peeled off from long soakings in water. It was an even bigger pain in winter, when the skin would peel off and the exposed red tender flesh could come into contact with many hairdressing products containing irritants. I overcame the pain by applying hand cream and wearing rubber gloves, and carried on with my work.

Army life had built up my body and will. But I missed my aged parents more and more as I had been away from them for years. The year 2003 was my first year working in the city. My boss didn't give me any Spring Festival leave, so I couldn't go back home to see my parents. That lonely Spring Festival was the least memorable in my life so far.

On the eve of the Chinese Lunar New Year, the hair salon was still crowded with customers. We worked until 1 in the morning. Our boss offered to treat us to a New Year dinner. But I was too tired to even drink water. I went to bed and fell asleep as soon as I got back to my rental room. I slept for two entire days.

When I woke up and opened my bleary eyes, it was 9 in the evening of the following day. I saw my sister Jianhong (adopted by my parents after my natural sister Weihua was lost) sitting beside me with tears running down her face. I learned that my parents had been calling me all day while I was sound asleep, and no one had answered the phone. They were so worried about me that they let my sister, who was working in a shoe factory in Wenzhou, to my home. My sister had not been able to wake me up no matter how hard she tried. She became frightened and burst into tears. My cell phone had run out of power through the countless calls from my parents.

That was the first Spring Festival that I spent outside my hometown. I remember my sister and I cooked noodle soup with eggs as our first "feast" of the new year. I came to the understanding that life was not easy, but that sometimes you really don't have a choice.

Family Reunion during the Spring Festival

This year's Spring Festival was the first I had spent together with my family since I began to work in the city. I attended a senior high school class reunion just before the Spring Festival. My former classmates talked of their wonderful university life, of Internet buzzwords, of popular electronic products, and of fashionable clothing brands. I felt like a misfit and just sat there smiling like a fool.

The class reunion was followed by a karaoke party. I got out of it by using the excuse that I wasn't feeling well. It was quite warm, but I still had on a pair of thick grey gloves as I shook hands with my classmates and said goodbye. They gave me one or two strange looks, but they didn't know that my hands, which should have been holding books and pens, had been disfigured by hairdressing products. During the whole of the 10 days I spent at home, I had been wearing the gloves for fear that my parents would be heartbroken and my former classmates would be scared. What I feared most was that I would be unable to hide my sadness from my family at the state of my hands, and that would ruin our rare family reunion.

After all, it was my own decision to work in the city. I know the path I have chosen is tough and I envy my classmates and friends who live a carefree life. But reality is ruthless. Those without a diploma can only live by their labor, and those without advanced skills will be exploited by their bosses. On the first day of the new year, I said to myself, "From this day forward, I will work hard and won't be distracted or affected by any obstacles on my way to success. The sun will smile on me every day."

I put this motto in the signature box of my QQ (popular Chinese chat software) account. The motto expresses my true feelings though the words are simple and straightforward. After this Spring Festival, I will head back south to the hair salon. This year, the salon will send a number of long-serving employees to training programs in Guangzhou, Guangdong. This will be a good opportunity for me.

Du Jianhong: Working on a Shoe Production Line

I'm Jianhong, 19 years old, Jianguo's sister. I never knew who my real parents were. Since I was very small, it was my foster parents who brought me up.

Dad and mom had always hoped I would study hard. But when I saw many of the girls in my class go to work in the cities, even though my grades were not bad, the idea of dropping out of school appealed to me. Before the senior high school entrance exam, with the help of a girl in my village I found work at a shoe factory in Wenzhou,

Zhejiang.

My adoptive parents have always treated me like their own daughter. They were strongly opposed to my going out to work at such a young age. But influenced by my classmates, I set my mind on earning money as early as possible to repay my parents for their loving care. I don't find work too painful, at least I don't feel mentally tired. My daily task is sticking labels onto shoes, threading shoelaces and packaging the shoes in different boxes according to the country or region where they will be sold.

But even an easy job will become a hard task after a thousand repetitions. Every day my fellow workers and I, all girls, sit by piles of shoes, sticking labels, threading shoelaces, and classifying and packing the shoes. After a time, everything we see looks like shoes to us and shoes often appear in our dreams.

At first I liked this simple way of life. My meals and accommodation are paid by the factory, so I can save 800 yuan a month out of my salary – slightly less than 1,000 yuan – and send it all to my parents.

Compared with boys of my age, we working girls seem to be more mature and more experienced in relationships. Many of my young fellow workers already have babies. For most of us girls working in the city, the major goals are to earn a dowry and to find a good opportunity to marry ourselves off. In a few years' time I will be a mother, too.

During Spring Festival this year, I learned that a close girlfriend from my village had been admitted to a leading university in Wuhan, Hubei. When we met back at home, we were no longer as intimate and relaxed as we used to be in junior high school. We just greeted each other with a slight smile and felt kind of embarrassed. She had the appearance of a student and looked rather intellectual. In the next few days following our meeting, I found myself thinking that I would have been like her if I had continued my schooling. But it was all my own choice, and it's already too late for regrets.

During the 20-day Spring Festival holiday, I registered for a short-term computer training course to learn basic typing and typesetting skills. In a couple of years' time when I have earned enough money, I will open up a printing shop. I have no great expectations that my life will be transformed in the years to come. My greatest goals are simply to bring up healthy kids and take good care of my parents. It is only recently that I have come to understand my parents' good intentions in urging me to study hard. Now I realize that studying is much more useful than I had thought, but it takes time for its worth to become apparent. Gaining knowledge can change one's destiny, even if the time it takes is long and the cost is high.

Tale of a Couple: Twenty Years of Toil

Narrator 1: Yang Shuangshuang, male, 46, from Huangpi District of Wuhan City, Hubei Province
Job: road builder – food stallholder – truck driver
Work place: Xinjiang Uyghur Autonomous Region – Wuhan

Narrator 2: Wang Qianlan, female, 42, wife of Yang Shuangshuang
Job: waste recycler
Work place: Wenzhou, Wuhan

Yang Shuangshuang: 20 Years of Life as a Migrant Worker

I was born in 1961, when China was suffering the last of the three years of natural disasters to which my three elder brothers and two sisters had borne witness.

When my elder brothers reached school age, they all had to go to work on the farm, but I was sent to school. Life in school was tough as there were no desks, no chairs, and not even any blackboards. Instead we had black wooden planks nailed to the wall. And every time I went to school, I had to take with me a tall square stool, which I used as a desk, and a small one to sit on. Besides attending school, I also had to do farm work for the family. I had some small but important tasks to complete every day: I got up early in the morning and collected pig and cow dung with my elder brothers before going to school; after school I grazed cows, moved millet, and cooked. So I didn't have much time for reviewing my lessons, and had no time and no energy to concentrate on my studies. I was often late for school, and was regularly punished as I rarely finished my homework. My poor academic performance and this constant loss of face gradually led me to detest school. But my parents were very strict with me and had high expectations. Because the whole family was illiterate, they hoped that I could study and become successful in order to escape the bonds of thousands of years of dung, dirt, and peasant family life. That was why my family forced me to go to school: for all that they were very poor.

I muddled through and became a middle-school student, in accordance with their wishes. The school was a long way from my home, so I took my lunch with me every day and cooked it in the school canteen. Some of my classmates from better-off families would bring things like sweet potatoes and eggs cooked with rice in their lunchboxes. I was part of a group of wayward boys who would always slip out of the classroom before lunch and go to the school canteen to rummage through our classmates' lunchboxes. If we found anything good, meat for example, we would share it. We didn't care who it belonged to. But those happy times didn't last long as the school soon got fed up with our misbehavior. Eventually we were expelled for causing disorder and giving the school a bad name. And so the school life that had been such a burden to me came to an end.

Building Roads in Xinjiang

At that time, life in rural areas was poor and eked out at subsistence level. Poverty was one of life's burdens to be endured. Young people relieved their frustration through alcohol, and idled their time away in the fields. Of course some people were diligent in their work – growing crops, laboring on their farms, and managing their living in a down-to-earth way. At that time, people's wants and needs were very simple – no more than being able to feed themselves.

I was forced to spend years in the fields grazing cows, and later baking bricks in a kiln. These jobs were physically demanding but brought no financial rewards. People in rural areas would normally get married before the age of 24. Most young people of my age already had their own children, two or three years old. But I "followed" the state policy of late marriage and late reproduction. I saw few prospects in my remote home village, and my only escape from the situation was to get out and find a job. Beyond that, I couldn't think of any way to break out of the cycle of poverty.

In 1985 I left the soil where I was born and grew up, and followed some experienced middle-aged men from neighboring villages to Ili in Xinjiang, to become a builder. I cast off the skills of transplanting rice seedlings, sowing, and harvesting, and threw myself into this strange new industry of construction in Xinjiang. My job was mainly to build roads and dig tunnels. It was dry in Xinjiang, and herds of sheep and cows on pasture lands were a common sight. Windstorms and sandstorms were frequent. Sometimes when a strong sandstorm filled the sky you couldn't even keep you eyes open. After the sandstorm passed your clothes would be saturated with a thick coating of sand. Life in those days was tough. Once we were assigned to an emergency project to build a road on a hillside. Since we only came back to our base camp once a week, before we left we would prepare enough steamed buns to last us for a whole week. As the week drew to a close, the remaining steamed buns got more and more stale, and they were hard to swallow even accompanied by water. Chewing our way through them, it felt like our throats were full of jagged lumps, and the pain was acute.

At the canteen on the construction site, my master let me into the secret of a full stomach: first, get a half bowl of rice and eat it quickly; then go back and get a full bowl. This was the way to get more rice and fill your belly. Previously, I had always taken a full bowl of rice first. By the time I had finished this and gone back for a second, the cauldron was always empty. I was surprised that those veteran workers were so cunning. I suppose their hard life taught them such lessons. But as more and more people cottoned on to the trick, it stopped working.

Tough and uneventful days succeeded each other in an unbroken routine....

One day when we were building a road at high altitude, the supervisor told us that we had to return to our base camp immediately, as there was going to be heavy snow in a couple of days – the road would be closed and the mountain would be cut off. So we collected up our shovels, buckets and belongings, and set off for home in a bus. It was late and the road was rough, and it was going to take 10 hours to drive from the mountain back to our camp. To keep out the cold, the Uyghur driver was drinking *baijiu*. He was drinking and driving at the same time, and none of us really understood the danger of drunken driving. Tired out, I fell asleep. Suddenly, I felt a heavy thump and heard the driver's loud cry: "Look out!" The bus turned over and fell to the bottom of a valley. All of us were terrified and had no idea what was happening. I was thrown out of the bus onto some stones, and lost my lower-middle tooth. Blood ran from my mouth and my face and body were covered with bruises. Some of my workmates suffered broken arms and ribs. What a disaster it was! I scared out of my wits. Fortunately, there were no fatalities.

After this frightening experience, and with the approach of the Lunar New Year, I decided to go home with my fellow villagers. But when I asked for my salary, the labor contractor went back on his word. He had told me he would pay me 20 yuan a day after taking out my living costs. But now he said he was only going to pay me 10 yuan a day for the whole four months. I went down on my hands and knees to him, and he finally gave me 1,600 yuan. For all my hard work, I had to go back to my hometown helpless, with a few hard-earned coins that were scant reward for the effort I had put in.

On my return to the village, my friends and family asked about my migrant worker life, and how much I had earned. When I told them that I had earned 1,600 yuan, their eyes boggled and their jaws dropped in shock. They couldn't have hoped to earn so much money in a whole year of farm work. They even asked me whether I could get jobs for their children. I didn't know what to say – they had no idea of the hardships a migrant worker had to endure. My mother set aside and saved 1,000 yuan for me from my first treasure trove, and the rest, a few hundred yuan, was spent on my living costs. Later, as more and more people became migrant workers, villagers agreed that going to school was a waste of time, while working away from home was an excellent way to earn money.

Around that time, all the able-bodied people in my village left to become migrant workers. They abandoned their homes and set off to make a living elsewhere. The only people who stayed behind in the village were the old, the sick, and the disabled – along with a few idle youths.

During my tough days as a migrant worker, my great dream was to join the army. As a vigorous and upright youth, I wanted to do my bit for the country, win respect, and become a hero. I had no fixed job and lacked a proper education, and I thought that joining the army would give me something worthwhile to do and improve my prospects.

Becoming a Migrant Worker in Wuhan

At the age of 26, I married an illiterate girl from a neighboring village. She gave birth to a boy and a girl. Now a husband, and father of two children, I couldn't allow myself to go to seed in this remote and backward village. So I made up my mind to go to the outside world, and decided that no matter what the future held for me, I would never come back to the village. I entrusted my children to my mother (my father having passed away), then I came to Wuhan with my wife.

The city was so different from the village: skyscrapers crowded into tight spaces; narrow streets crowded with vehicles and people; colorful lights filling the city's night sky. I felt invigorated – everything about the city was so exciting. At the same time I subjected myself to a barrage of questions: in this sea of migrant workers, was I going to be able to find a job and feed my family?

Although I was both excited and hesitant, I started my first business – roasting Chinese chestnuts. I would normally set up my stall beside malls and prosperous fairs. With luck, I could earn 40 or 50 yuan a day. One day, a vehicle carrying the words "City Management Bureau" appeared out of nowhere and seized my stall. After that I changed my job frequently, working as a breakfast seller, porter, motorized tricycle rider, cart puller, owner of waste recycling station, and truck driver. My life began to follow a more normal routine through these life experiences. I was able to save a little money; I rose early and went to bed late, and worked diligently at my business for 20 years. Now, as a long-distance truck driver in Wuhan, I've bought my own truck, and help people deliver goods. My wife runs a waste recycling station, so I also spend a lot of time carrying waste books and paper to paper mills.

My long-distance business destinations are Yueyang in Hunan Province or Xinyang in Henan Province. But I often get tired and short of energy as I am now nearly 50 years old. I suffer from high blood pressure – something that used to be called a "rich man's disease" back in my home village. I am a little overweight, and have a weather-beaten face with sunken and swollen eyes.

As a truck driver, I have had some disheartening experiences.

Once on a trip to Hunan I drove for a day and a night without stop. Exhaustion set in, and I couldn't carry on – I was plagued with cold sweats and discomfort. I took a few pills to lower my high blood pressure, and ignoring the pain I drove the truck to a roadside rest stop. I clung to the steering wheel and took a break. After 10 minutes or so the discomfort receded and I began to feel a little better. When I looked up, I saw a white slip posted on my front windshield. I had been fined 200 yuan for illegal parking. People who have never been through this kind of thing have no idea of the heavy load a farmer driver has to bear to make a living.

During my 20 years as a migrant worker, my son and daughter have grown up. Nowadays there is a special name for children like mine – "leftover children." My daughter is a student at a normal university and my son, in his third year at high school, is approaching the university entrance exam. I feel his pressure – all my hopes are invested in my children. I hope they will succeed as quickly as possible in getting rid of their rural identities and becoming real urban residents, never to suffer the hardships I have endured. Although I have made an honest living for most of my life, I am still in poverty. My farmer identity reminds me that I still don't belong to this city, and we remain "outsiders."

As time passes, I have become weary of the crowds and the din of the city, and I detest the way that people intrigue against each other. Gradually, I begin to miss the open lands of my home and the modest folk ways of my fellow villagers. But I know only too well that my poor home village can't compete with the affluent and prosperous city. I'm not obsessed with money, but money is useful. I need money to pay for the cost of my children's daily life and education, to improve my own living conditions, and to live a comfortable life.... I know only too well that my monthly salary is not enough for a man like me with a family to keep. But the temptations of the outside world have already bound me to life in the city.

Wang Qianlan: Wife of a Rural Migrant Worker

When I was a child, I was very diligent and good at housework. I had four siblings who all finished their primary school, but I was told that I had to stay at home to help my parents and wasn't to go to school at all. I defied my parents about this and quarreled with them, refusing to do any housework. After I had stayed in bed for two days to express the strength of my feelings, my parents had to send me to school. I was assigned to the pre-school class with my brother who was six years younger than me. I felt embarrassed at finding myself attending the same class as those little brothers and sisters. I worked very hard in my first class, and my teacher praised me for my neat and beautiful handwriting. But after only two days at the bottom of the class, I left. Although I was desperate not to miss out on the opportunity of studying, I had to face reality.

Illiteracy destroyed my expectations for the future. Perhaps my life would be the same as other women in my village: married early, have a baby, then become a housewife spending her time on farm work, worrying about the crops and penny-pinching for food.... I was scared to work elsewhere as I was afraid of being abducted. I was sure that because I was illiterate I would be stuck in my village forever.

Running a Waste Recycling Station

Later, I married. I was not prepared to spend my whole life

working on a farm, so I came to the city with my husband and became a migrant worker too. In the beginning things went badly, and we seemed to have run into a brick wall. Because of our rural accents we were mocked as "country bumpkins" by the city dwellers. With little education, we had to take on laboring jobs that didn't require any academic skills. But even though life was hard, we still earned better money than we had done back in the village. Later, things started to improve. Now I run a waste recycling station in the city, and my husband makes money driving our own delivery truck.

On one occasion my illiteracy cost me dear. A woman with whom I had traded for some time came to buy our goods. She said she was short of money and didn't have enough to pay for the goods in cash. So she gave me an IOU on which the sum was written out in Chinese characters. I didn't check the IOU, as we knew each other well. Later, when she came to pay the IOU which should have been for 7,400 yuan, she deceitfully claimed that it was only 4,700 yuan. She boldly told me to show her the IOU. The result was easy to see. She had deliberately written it that way because she knew I was illiterate. I was cheated out of my hard-earned savings. I fell ill as a result of the incident. My illiteracy cost me money, caused me great distress, and made me distrustful of other people.

I have heard many stories about migrant workers who resort to radical methods to get their hard-earned money back. Some have committed suicide by jumping off a building; others have attacked or threatened project contractors who owe them money. Perhaps their behavior seems uneducated, stupid, excessive, or disgraceful in the eyes of townspeople, but you have no idea of our struggle for existence unless you've been one of us. We know nothing about the law and are even intimidated by the doors of the courts. We wish that wider society could see our point of view and be more inclusive toward us.

In my opinion, as a married woman I should manage my life carefully, be loyal to my family, trust my husband, work hard, feed our children, and help my husband realize his dreams and mine. I do believe that life is full of hope as long as we remain diligent and honest.

Two Years in Shenzhen

Narrator: Zhang Xiaolan, female, 39, from Niefan Village of Jingmen City, Hubei Province
Job: worker in a toy factory
Work place: Shenzhen, Guangdong Province

Last year I worked as a migrant worker in Shenzhen and came home after this Spring Festival. My husband manages eight *mu* of dry farmland in my home village. We harvest wheat in spring and cotton in autumn.

I came from a poor family, and married my husband in 1986. We didn't have our own home until our daughter was three years old. We had to share a small house with his brother. After a couple of years' struggle, we obtained a loan to build our own house with the help of my parents.

In the summer of 2004, my son suffered from stomach pains for several days, and a swelling appeared under the skin over his kidney. His father took him to the village clinic where the doctor diagnosed a bloated stomach and said that my son just needed a few injections. However, when my son came home after the injections he was still in terrible pain and rolled around on the floor in agony. We were scared and immediately sent him to the county hospital for a physical examination. The examination result suggested that my son was suffering from a congenital kidney perforation. He needed treatment for more than a month in hospital at a cost of over 10,000 yuan. At that time, the annual income of our family was 4,000 to 5,000 yuan. So, we had debts of more than 8,000 yuan.

That same summer, the whole family was delighted when his elder sister passed the university entrance exam, but we didn't know how to pay her tuition fees of over 8,000 yuan. As a considerate daughter, she proposed to leave the village and become a migrant worker. Her father and I rejected this idea. We had gone through all sorts of hardship to help her pass the university entrance exam, and we were determined that she should go to university whatever the cost. I had a discussion with her father and we came to a decision: I would go out to work and let her go to university. When she went to university, my daughter took only a little money for her daily needs. As for the tuition fees, we crossed our fingers that the future would provide a solution. My own life offered little prospect of happiness, but I had to make it through for my son and daughter. I was told that female migrant workers were needed in Shenzhen, so I left for Shenzhen with a group of others and stayed there for two years.

I had never previously considered coming to Shenzhen. I was afraid of leaving my home village because I had been told that there were many kidnappers elsewhere. I didn't know what I would do if I couldn't find a job, as I didn't have enough money to buy a return ticket. I was reluctant to leave the family as our farm was hard for my husband to manage on his own. And my son had not yet fully recovered and had to be fed by an intestinal tube. There would be no-one to take care of him if I left home. Huanying, a fellow villager who was a migrant worker for several years and now introduces workers to her employer for a fee of 300 yuan for each successful introduction, told me that her employer needed new recruits. So with her help I signed up and she brought us to Shenzhen.

As a supervisor Huanying also had a hard job, as she had to run a lot of risk. The toy factory in Shenzhen was recruiting female workers between the ages of 18 and 28. Generally, women over 30 like us would not be taken on. However, Huanying could solve this problem through collecting ID cards from younger women and applying for false ID cards in the household register department in the police station (she had connections there). Minor differences in age and appearance would not cause a problem as she also had connections in the factory. I remember that the ID card she used for me belonged to a 28-year-old woman from a neighbor village. Once she had given me the ID card, she asked me for 138 yuan for my train ticket. I borrowed the money from her and told her that I would pay her back as soon as I got my first salary. So my arrangements were made.

Three days later, under Huanying's guidance, I boarded the train to Shenzhen with my fellow villagers. This was my first ever train journey, and I was excited. Following the crowd of passengers like a sheep, I made my way to the carriage. I quickly found a seat thanks to my slight build and my scant luggage. The women chatted warmly on the train. I wasn't actually aware of the fact when the train arrived in Shenzhen. I simply carried on following the crowd, walking when they walked and stopping when they stopped. I had no idea where we were going, until we arrived at the gate of the toy factory.

My First Impression of Shenzhen

Shenzhen made a huge impression on me as it was the first time I had ever traveled any distance from my home. As soon as we got off the train we were surrounded by crowds of people. I was confronted by a scene of hustle and bustle. The whole station was packed with all sorts of people in colorful clothes, carrying baggage of all shapes and sizes. People approached us, asking where we were headed and whether we needed tickets. Before I had any idea what was happening, Huanying had driven them off.

We got off the bus and followed Huanying as if we were walking through a maze. The streets were lined with factories – cotton mills, towel factories, garment factories and food factories. Groups of factories producing all sorts of daily commodities are gathered together offering coordinated services. For example, cotton yarn is woven into fabrics in cotton mills, and then dyed, printed and processed into towels, garments and blankets as needed.

The clatter of machinery, the sound of truck horns, and the noise of people combined to create a sense of business and prosperity. The sky was grey and the hot sun scorched the cement below your feet and burned them. Trees were scarce, and only a few large potted plants by the entrances of big stores offered some decoration. High walls enclosed factories all around – the factory we were heading for also lay hidden behind such walls.

The jobs in the toy factory comprised component assembly, painting and packing. There were several workshops to deal with the three processes, and the pay scales were different. Each production line was staffed by several female workers under the administration of a supervisor.

We entered the factory through the back door and went to the personnel department. The procedures were very complicated and all of us were hungry and tired. We waited for two or three hours, and eventually Huanying came out with a list of assignments. We were faint with hunger as we hadn't eaten anything at all that day, so we hoped to get something into our bellies as soon as possible.

There were five of us, including three from my village. I was assigned to the assembling workshop with Xiuzhen, one of my two fellow villagers. The other, named Aizhi, was assigned to the packaging workshop. The two women from the neighboring village were assigned to the paint spraying workshop. Huanying told us that we would be paid on a piece rate basis. Salaries in the packaging and paint spraying workshops were a little higher; workers in the packaging workshop, where the work was easier, got their jobs through connection with the factory; jobs in the paint spraying workshop were tiring and dirty but the pay was higher. My salary was not too bad as long as I could keep up a good rate of work. In fact I would have liked a better-paid job in the packaging workshop where Aizhi was working – I didn't care much about whether the work was tiring or not.

Then we followed Huanying to our dormitory, which was several minutes' walk from our workplace. The dormitory was surrounded by residential buildings, grocery stores and garment stores, which kept the noise down. We could buy all our daily needs by the gates of the dormitory. The grocery store where we often shopped was called Guangfulai; its owner was a sociable local resident.

We got to the dormitory around dusk. Spinners, printers and garment workers lived in a dozen or so seven-floor buildings that had been built jointly by several factory owners. We lived on the fourth floor of the No.6 building, which was inhabited by workers from our factory. There were 12 rooms on each floor and 10 people shared each room. The whole room covered about 20 sq m and was filled with five bunk beds and a large wardrobe. It was very hot in summer as there were no electric fans and no air conditioners. I was happy to stay in the factory as it was equipped with air conditioners. Living in a room like an oven, I had to buy a hand fan to try to keep cool. We couldn't sleep due to the temperature, which could rise to over 40 degrees Celsius, and the whine of mosquitoes. It was hard to fall asleep unless you were exhausted; inevitably you would wake up soaked in sweat.

Winter was better than summer, but with so many people sharing a small room we would often quarrel with each other over trifles.

Once when I came back to the dormitory, I was questioned by one of my roommates from Guizhou who had lost her new stockings. I told her I had never seen them. She cried out in rage, accusing me of having stolen the stockings because there was only one person in the room when she came back with the stockings, and that person was me. I was angry, and a fierce quarrel ensued. I hadn't stolen her stockings, and I didn't take kindly to the manner of her questioning. Eventually it was Xiuzhen who separated us. Not a word was exchanged between us for several days. She later found her stockings in a corner, but never offered the slightest apology to me. As a result, I never spoke to her again as long as I worked in the factory.

Working on the Production Line

Many rural migrant workers will tell you how unscrupulous their bosses are when they come back home. New recruits in our factory have to work for a month on probation, for which they will be paid half of the going rate (which comes to only about 300 yuan for the month). If they accept this, they will be paid their first salary a month in arrears, to make sure they don't take the money and run. If they don't accept it, they will never see their first month's salary. Workers in our factory are paid 0.03 yuan for each toy assembled, so we can earn a maximum of about 700 yuan in a month. We sit on a chair for 10 hours per day, and stretch ourselves when we go to toilet. Anyone who goes to the toilet too often is reprimanded by the supervisors. How exasperating for us, women in our thirties, to be disciplined by these young supervisors! As a result, we seldom go to toilet. After long days sitting on a chair, our buttocks become calloused. At the height of summer we develop heat rashes, causing itching and pain.

When I was at home I lived a free life; I could work at a pace that suited me and take a rest when I needed. Now I had to work from dawn till dusk without sufficient rest. When I came back to the dormitory at night, my whole body ached. I could hardly raise my arms, and fell asleep as soon as my head hit the pillow – too old for such a life, unlike the youngsters, full of energy all day long.

Our meals were provided by the factory, and a special canteen was set up in the courtyard of the dormitory area. I had only had some steamed buns and gruel before going to work on my first day. You had to watch and learn by yourself as no one would teach a new recruit how to do the job. The production line on which I was working was mainly responsible for assembling toys from components. Workers sitting on both sides of the production line were responsible for successive operations. The parts each one needed were supplied to us, and the supervisor added more as required.

When we went to the factory, we had to wear our uniforms: long-sleeved blouses and trousers. There are several production lines in each workshop. Each supervisor, who is a local resident or a relative of the boss, takes charge of several lines. They are paid over 1,000 yuan a month. The workshop directors have higher salaries, about 3,000 to 4,000 yuan a month excluding bonuses and dividends. I hope that my daughter will one day get such a comfortable and well-paid job.

Jobs on the production lines are unstable as the factory is not very profitable. During slack seasons there isn't much work to do. We would work for two and half hours in the afternoon and earn perhaps 500 to 600 yuan a month. During busy seasons the factory would order us to work overtime for a couple of hours, so we would get a higher salary at the end of the month. However, this is very tiring when you're not sleeping well. At one point I had lost five kilograms in weight. But I didn't care whether the work was boring or not as long as I could earn money for my daughter's daily needs.

This past year, my highest monthly salary was 700 yuan and my average salary was about 500 to 600 yuan. I was able to save about 400 yuan a month after my own needs were taken care of. I mailed money to my family every three months. I had never written letters before, but over the year I wrote several letters to my husband filled with trivia about my life.

I once told him in a letter that I was not used to the food and had lost a lot of weight. That Spring Festival my husband asked someone to bring me a big bag of fried peanuts, and some dried fish. I could imagine how hard he had worked to shell such peanuts.

I didn't go home for Spring Festival as a ticket was hard to come by and it was also expensive. I thought I would rather mail 100 yuan to my family than buy a ticket. I had no idea how my husband was spending his Spring Festival at home.

Life in Guangdong

The Cantonese like to put sugar in their food, and eat sweet soups before a meal. If there is no soup prepared before a meal, they will dilute some broth with hot water and drink it. I am completely unused to dishes with sugar added.

The climate here is comfortable, with moderate temperatures and lots of rain. Sweaters and quilted jackets are unnecessary at any time of the year. All sorts of fruits are available throughout the year. I tasted pitaya, longan and lychee for the first time.

Using your meal tickets, you could buy steamed buns, rice porridge and sweet pickled radishes in the canteen for breakfast. But there was little rice in the porridge, and the soft, white steamed buns tasted bland and felt like a piece of sponge to the touch. Lunch always consisted of rice and vegetables. During the holidays our meals would improve. For example, during the Spring Festival our factory manager and foreign boss would pay an inspection visit and make speeches, telling us that our meals would be improved to welcome the coming of a new year. Then the canteen would provide some tasty dishes, and each of us would get a plump chicken leg. These tasted like sawdust, but they were still the best food we were ever offered in the canteen.

We were very busy during the Spring Festival, and it took several nights of overtime to complete our work. I had planned to knit a sweater for my son, but I was busy at work from morning to night. By the time I had enough time to knit a sweater, it was already too warm. Later, my son told me that my younger brother's wife had made one for him. My young sister-in-law is kind; she took good care of my son and daughter. She also made cotton-padded shoes for both of them when they were babies.

Generally, we had to work in factory and had no time for leisure. During slack seasons, when we got off work earlier than usual, we could take a shower in the dormitory and go window-shopping at the night market. We rarely bought anything as we were afraid of being overcharged. Owners of clothes stores would ignore your age and call out, "Come in and take a look, you handsome boys and pretty girls!" We were flattered by their words, but we also knew they would show no mercy when bargaining with us. They would charge unbelievable prices to you if they knew you were not locals. Some Cantonese would even beat up non-local customers. So we dared not venture too far from the dormitory.

Security was not good there, and street fights and robberies were common. Xiuqin told me that rich women wearing gold necklaces and earrings and carrying purses and mobile phones were often robbed by people riding motorcycles. They would lose their belongings before they knew what was happening. Some victims' ears were torn in the process. It was dangerous to go out at night, so we would take a stroll in the vicinity of our dormitory, and then go home.

Thanks to the good water and the soil, Cantonese people have a fair complexion. I looked as white as the urban residents after I had been there for a few months. During the holidays, some large supermarkets would place big potted plants at their doors. On the day of the Mid-autumn Festival, a supermarket called Jiajiafu put several expensive orange trees at their entrance. Xiuzhen stealthily picked an orange as we passed — they were so big and ripe. I didn't do that because I thought that it was wrong to take something that didn't belong to me.

The buildings near our dormitory were inhabited by Cantonese whom we rarely saw. They were extravagant, and often discarded nearly-new clothes which had been worn only once. How shameless they were! We didn't even buy new clothes for the Spring Festival. I couldn't tolerate this kind of waste. Sometimes, I would have liked to pick up those nearly-new clothes, but I was afraid of being ridiculed by the others.

My fellow villagers Xiuzhen and Aizhi were my best friends, and we often went out together. Gradually, we got to know the owner of a grocery store which we frequented. She often talked about her family. She told us that she had a daughter and a son. Her mother-in-law had become kinder to her after she gave birth to her son. "The damned old thing used to nag me for not giving birth to a boy; now she's happy as she has the grandson she wanted." Most Cantonese prefer boys to girls.

Everyone Has Changed

An old Chinese saying goes that "We rely on relatives when at home and depend on friends when outside." It's not till you leave home that you really understand the meaning of this old saying. Some of my roommates were good at organizing groups of fellow villagers. Those from Guizhou Province are the most fashionable and they love to show off on meals and clothes; people from Sichuan Province are the most diligent and many Sichuan couples come out to find jobs; people from Hubei are considered to be the most cunning.

Girls from Guizhou were lively, and they chatted for the most of the night when they came back to the dormitory. We middle-aged women who were overwhelmed by the workload had no energy left to chat. The young girls were always dressing like coquettes, and they always owned all sorts of cosmetics like eyebrow pencils and face puffs. They would gather together and chat when they were at work. They were always changing their clothes according to the latest fashion, while we never bought new clothes unless old ones were worn out.

People who lived in the same dormitory building didn't usually talk unless they knew each other. If someone upstairs poured water out of the window, the downstairs residents would shout out in protest, and face-to-face quarrels would sometimes result. Fortunately, I had Xiuzhen and some other close friends.

Xiuzhen had contracted Hepatitis B when she was in the village. She was found out and fired after a few months in the factory, and she had to go home alone. From the beginning Aizhi didn't care for Xiuzhen and hated to put her chopsticks anywhere near Xiuzhen's. She would not go to the mess hall with Xiuzhen, and eventually stopped talking to her at all. Under the influence of Aizhi, other roommates also turned against Xiuzhen. Finally she had to wrap her plate in a plastic bag and keep it in a corner of the cupboard. She even had to go to the canteen alone. But I liked to talk to her and she would share her problems with me.

Xiuzhen's family was poor, and she had to cater for her parents and her two sons, who were in middle school. Her husband was an alcoholic, and would lose his temper and break pots and plates unless he was supplied with alcohol. Her family's farmlands were not managed well, so, she had to go out and become a migrant worker. What a wretched woman Xiuzhen was! She always took a few extra steamed buns as she said she often felt hungry. She had a good appetite even though she didn't look strong. Xiuzhen was a hard worker with the best productivity in her workshop.

Whenever she talked to me she always wanted to talk about her sons. I knew she missed them very much. So did I. Sometimes, when people told me that I was wanted on the phone by my family, I was too excited to say anything to them when I actually picked up the phone.

Aizhi was a pretty woman with a husband in our village. Her looks improved with city life. Her skin grew fair and she looked just like an urban resident when she dressed up. She was full of guile and never gave in to anybody about anything. She was also somewhat two-faced – she might flatter you to your face and disparage you behind your back. At first she behaved herself, but after three moths she had an affair with the director of her workshop. She told me that the director was going to increase her salary and promote her to supervisor of the production line. Every day she would dress herself in fancy clothes. I don't know whether her Cantonese male-friend kept his word. I don't know whether she was promoted, as I left the factory.

There was a slim, dark-skinned woman from Sichuan Province who always looked sickly. She had come to Shenzhen with her husband. I was told that they had been classmates in high school and both of them failed the university entrance exam. I saw her handsome husband. They didn't have a marriage license, but they were regarded as a couple as they had held a marriage banquet in their home village. At first they were close. But two or three months later the man ran off with a female boss from Taiwan. As the woman wept in the dormitory, we came to realize that she was several months pregnant. Her husband should be damned. She had to have an abortion, and we never found out how her life turned out after that.

People change quickly, and no one knows what's going on in other people's heads. Many of those who leave their hometowns go on to change a lot. Needless to say, like my fellow villagers who accompanied me to work away from home, I also changed a lot. Sometimes I would ask myself if I had done the right thing in going away to work.

Some of the girls in our factory were quiet at first. But after a period of time, they would be rushing around as if the only thing they were interested in was boys. Many of the girls around the age of 18 were flighty, not at all like their peers in our village.

To be honest, I was unwilling to leave Shenzhen after two years of being a migrant worker there. Urban residents did not treat us particularly well, and some of them looked down upon us. My job was tiring and the pay was poor. Nevertheless, life in a city is more comfortable than life in a village with respect to food, clothes and other daily necessities. And as long as I was willing to work hard, I could save a little money at the end of the month. Back home, I will have no disposable income unless I can sell every ounce of the cotton we produce. I would like to be an urban resident. I don't want to see my son and daughter end up like me, wearing themselves out for a few coppers. But I have had to come back to my village to tend the farm, and it is impossible for me to return to the city.

Making Better Neon Signs

Narrator: Zhang Tieniu, male, 22, from Xiaoxi Yeying Village of Hengshui City, Hebei Province
Job: welder – flyer distributor – neon sign maker
Work place: Hengshui, Hebei Province

I'm the son of an ordinary farmer, but I have high hopes for my future.

In September 1998, I was enrolled into No.10 Middle School of Hengshui. At that time, I was ambitious and was determined to enter a good high school. I studied very hard. Although my English was moderate, I often tried to memorize words from a notebook on the way to school.

Two months before the entrance examination to senior high school, a shocking event brought turmoil to my life, and had a significant impact on my studies. One April day, my father went to work as usual at a local power substation. His task that day was to repair electrical wire in a building housing a motor-pumped well. During the afternoon, while he was still at work, one of his colleagues turned on some power switches. He should have turned on the circuits whose wire had been repaired; instead he turned on the one that my father was still repairing. A powerful 380-voltage current struck my father. He fell from a metal pylon and landed on the roof of the building below, then fell down from the roof.

Although my father survived, I was traumatized by the incident and could not concentrate on my studies. I went to school every day still aspiring to go on to senior high school, but I did not make progress. My exam results put an end to my hopes. When my parents asked me whether I would like to go to a vocational school, I thought of our financial situation and said "No," though I was in internal conflict. The truth was that I did want to continue my studies. But my hopes had to give way to reality.

After my father had been discharged from hospital, he stayed at home to recuperate. I took care of him. Our relationship improved, and I felt relieved as his health improved. By the end of 2001 he was better, and I had to find work. I followed my father to work on village meters that record electricity used for irrigation. The weather was poor, always snowy or foggy. But every morning we got up at six and walked for more than two hours to the workplace. At noon we ate steamed stuffed buns and then worked. In the evening, we walked home in darkness.

Father hoped I could learn gas welding. He believed that acquiring new skills should never be seen as a burden, and that I would have better prospects of a good job if I learnt this trade. But I didn't like welding; the heat was scorching and my skin got burnt. I wanted to be an electrician; it was cleaner work. My mother wouldn't listen to me. "Electricity is dangerous – you can't see it," she said. "Just look at what happened to your father!" My mind was in a state of tumult; I knew that my parents wanted what was best for me, but they just couldn't see things from my point of view.

On the morning of August 22, 2003, my father was suffering from a headache. He asked me to fetch him some painkillers.

Mother and I tried to persuade him to go to hospital, but he refused, saying, "No need to go to hospital. I'll be OK once I've taken some medicine." In fact, he had been suffering from stress for more than a week, drinking a bottle of 53° *baijiu* almost every day. He took the medicine and went to work. But after a short while the headache became unbearable, and he decided to come home on his motorbike. Unfortunately, on the way he fainted and crashed in a cornfield to the east of our village. Some villagers saw what had happened and quickly let me know. I borrowed an electric three-wheeler and hurried to the field. On the way to hospital, Father could not say a word, and he grasped my hand tightly. I could feel him trembling, and one side of his body had turned stiff. That half hour seemed to go on for ever. I could think of nothing but my Father.

Father was admitted into an emergency ward and put on an intravenous drip. As they pushed him in on a rolling bed, the doctor said he was at death's door. I was shocked. We signed the necessary forms with the hospital and the doctors made one last attempt to save Father. But he left us for ever. I wept so loudly that I lost my voice. I could not believe what had happened.

First Job at an Advertising Company

A month after Father passed away, I still did not want to work, and sat staring blankly at Father's portrait for days on end. Finally one of his friends helped me find a job with the Hengxin Advertising Company in Hengshui City. I was responsible for welding the steel frames of outdoor billboards, having learnt the basics from my father, so I was a reasonably competent welder. The working hours were irregular. We were usually busiest on weekends and holidays when others were enjoying their leisure. At first I found the job tough, and the boss was constantly criticizing and reprimanding me.

I sweated blood every day, for what would be a salary of only 400 yuan a month. But I was not bothered about the money; I wanted to improve myself. After work, I began to apply myself to a number of new skills, including typing. I wasn't familiar with even the basic functions of computers, and turned to colleagues for help. My aim was to become a programmer in a sizable company, and escape from working outdoors. But my hopes were soon dashed: I contracted a serious illness after only a few weeks at my new job.

In October, I went back to Hengxin. Then the boss announced that the company had too many staff and that productivity was not good enough. He let us know that he was going to fire some people, and mentioned me by name, saying that I wasn't doing a good job. So I quit.

I got along well with one of the other employees at Hengxin, A Xing. He introduced me to a store near the People's Park. In November, I went to work at this store selling advertising materials. The monthly salary was 400 yuan and the store provided lunch. So I had a new position. But the manager constantly complained and found fault with me, however well I did.

No matter how busy I was, I was always on the lookout for a better job and a chance to acquire new skills.

In the summer of 2004, I started to work at Sanying Neon Shop. I worked very hard there, but was not well rewarded for my efforts.

In July, my boss and I went to Fucheng County to install advertising characters for a feed mill. Our work was to install the name of the mill onto a 21-m-high square pillar standing among the mill workshops. Each character, three m long and two m high, was composed of several components. We had to install them one by one.

We had a hoist with a basket, but my boss and I were working alone. We stood together in the basket as it hung in the air. As I tried to drill the wall, the electric drill would bounce back causing the basket to swing back and forth. I had to wait till the basket became stable again to continue my drilling. It took time and a lot of effort. On the second day, in order to meet the work schedule, I asked my uncle and cousin to help us. They worked on the roof – this was more dangerous since they had nothing to hold on to, and if they were not careful they might fall from a considerable height. Under these conditions we worked for more than 12 hours per day, installing 15 characters on three sides of the pillar.

My boss had promised to pay us well. The three of us worked hard. But to my disappointment, we got only 30 yuan per day.

Hard Days in a Workshop

After the Spring Festival in 2005, my mother heard that welders at the Haijiang Press Filter Factory could earn more than 1,000 yuan per month. She wanted me to give it a try. At that time the factory was recruiting, and many young men scrambled for jobs there. One of my cousin's schoolmates introduced me to the factory. I did not sign any labor contract, and had to pay the factory 100 yuan to buy a work uniform.

I worked in the mold shop, where there were about 20 workers. As a newcomer, I learned welding and cutting from skilled workers. I had to repeatedly squat and then stand up, causing my back and my waist to ache. And welding and cutting was dangerous. Carelessness might result in flareback, which in turn could cause the oxygen and acetylene cylinders to explode. Even in such dangerous circumstances I could not get good work, and earned only around 400 yuan each month.

I was often dissatisfied, and could not get satisfactory work at the factory. In six months I earned only a little more than 2,000 yuan. In September, I quit and decided to return to advertising.

Back to the Advertising Business

A friend introduced me to New City Media Advertising Company. There were seven to eight similar companies in Hengshui City. This company's business covered mainly urban Hengshui, and its advertising circulation reached 10,000. At first, I distributed fliers, walking around the city and covering every high street and back lane. Then I was given the responsibility of finding potential clients, something that could help improve my articulacy and personal qualities. In this highly competitive field, among so many competent people, it would take outstanding personal attributes to carve a space for myself.

I cycled around the city every day, trying to find advertisers, mainly new shops. After a couple of weeks, I realized that the advertising market in Hengshui was small, and very competitive, and thus it was difficult for advertising companies to grow. I wanted to find something new, with more potential.

I borrowed 50 yuan from a friend and took a train to Shijiazhuang at 5 o'clock one morning. I traveled around Shijiazhuang by bus, hoping to find a job making neon signs. At noon, I found a neon company and inquired about the prospects. It turned out my sign-making skills were far from unique, and offered no great potential. I had planned to spend some time in Shijiazhuang, find a place to live, learn some more advanced skills, and broaden my horizons. But at the end of the day I went home with nothing.

In October, a friend who had studied graphic design opened an advertising company, and so I went to work with him. I knew little about computers. To learn graphic design, I first had to learn typing. I bought a teaching device for 60 yuan. I kept practicing typing till my fingers ached. But to master this basic skill, I forced myself to continue practicing. I trained for more than a month, and eventually became a capable typist. I had overcome the first obstacle. Then I applied myself to learning Photoshop. I turned to colleagues for help whenever I encountered difficulties. But they were busy with their own work and did not want to spend time training me. I decided to buy a book and study by myself. By December, I thought I had learned all I could at the advertising company, and wanted to quit.

I was always looking to learn something useful, and was anxious for success. But it always turned out that the more haste, the less speed. For example, when learning to use software, I really needed to understand its components, their functions and how to apply them. It was all about details. But I refused to give up. I could ask others, or try again and again by myself. I continued to pursue my goals.

My Dream – Making My Own Neon Signs

In December 2005, one of my friends took on the job of making and installing a neon sign for a tobacco and liquor shop. But he was too busy so he passed the job on to me. I accepted. It was the first time I had produced a neon sign independently. I designed a sample sign based on the requirements of the client, who gave me 500 yuan up front. As I had no experience, I ended up buying the things I needed bit by bit when I needed them in the process. The advance wasn't enough for me to buy all the materials. Without enough money,

I had to ask for help and buy on credit. I had all sorts of problems before I finally connected up the wiring. But then I found something was wrong with a control unit. I had to go to the supplier and change it several times.

The client did not pay me immediately after I finished the job. I asked for my money more than 20 times. I knew that he wouldn't pay me the first time. So I went to his place again and again, with no results. What was I going to do if he didn't pay me? The loss was too big to contemplate. I thought it over and decided to talk to the client gently. The new strategy worked. He finally paid me, though 400 yuan less than I had been promised. But I had to accept. Better than nothing.

I earned more than 300 yuan from that first independent job. I reviewed the experience and found that I had learned a lot about the process of making neon signs, gathering valuable experience for future work. The biggest lesson was that I had not signed a contract with the client, and when I asked for payment I had no proof. This taught me that next time I would ask the client to pay 30% of the total payment in advance and sign a contract stating that the balance would be paid after I completed the work. As the saying goes, fall in a pit, gain in wit.

After the Spring Festival in 2006 I decided to start my own business. But no matter how long I had spent learning my trade, and how much I knew, I was still starting from scratch. Everything demands courage. For nearly five years, from 2001 to 2006, I had worked for others, being taken advantage of and suffering wrongs as a consequence. It would be better if I worked for myself. After careful consideration, I decided to launch my own business and realize my neon dream.

In March 2006, I turned my log-held ambition into reality. I scraped together 10,500 yuan in start-up capital: I borrowed 2,500 yuan from my brother, 5,000 yuan from my aunt, 1,000 yuan from my neighbor, and added 2,000 yuan of my own. I invested 3,500 yuan on a computer; 800 yuan on a scanner, a printer and a computer desk; 680 yuan on two titanium plates used to make characters; 180 yuan on an electric drill; 230 yuan on a cutter; 380 yuan on an electric hammer; 80 yuan on a polishing machine; 150 yuan on a ladder; 100 yuan on tin solder; and 3,000 yuan on a year's rental. I decided to use the rest to buy materials.

On March 4, I started my own business in my rented store. It was about 20 sq m, on Yongxing Road in Hengshui City. The rental for my store was cheaper than others as there were two drain pipes and two exhaust ducts inside the premises. At first the sound of running water got on my nerves. Particularly when it came to summer, the noise seemed to go on all night and I could hardly get to sleep. Alas! I had only wanted to save a little money. But as time passed I gradually got used to the noise. Sometimes, exhausted after working a whole day, I would fall asleep immediately, hearing nothing at all.

A Chinese saying provided a good start for a new business. My first job was not bad, making a 4.5-m-long, 5.5-m-high neon sign for a nightclub. According to the contract, I would be able to earn 1,800 yuan. But after I had produced and installed the sign, the client said it was crooked. I had to take it down and check it. It turned out that one of the angle bars on the steel support was crooked, and I hadn't noticed when making the sign. I had to weld the steel again. I was afraid of missing the deadline as the club needed the sign for its opening ceremony. I was so nervous that I worked day and night. The night before the club's opening, I managed to finish the sign, and set it down outside the front of my store. To make sure it didn't get stolen, I kept the door open and the lights on, and slept on the floor near the door. The night was short. It seemed that I had just fallen asleep when day broke. I got up quickly, called a hoist and rushed to the club to install the sign. The hoist lifted up the sign and I did the drilling and welding. I worked until around eight o'clock in the morning. It was hard going and I had only slept for about three hours the night before. But finally I could relax.

During that first job I hit some snags, but I was proud because I had done everything myself from beginning to end, right down to the very last detail. Moreover, the client paid me immediately after I finished the job. So I was optimistic about the prospects of a bright future.

Toward the end of November, I accepted a more challenging job: to make and install a giant billboard for a travel agency. The board was 11 m high and 1.5 m wide – I had never installed such a big one before. On November 20, after signing a contract with the agency, I set straight to work. But during the first few days, when I had planned to buy materials, it was either snowing or raining. It was not until the 26th that I started to make the billboard. I finished it on December 2, using more than 120 m of neon tubes. It was difficult to install such a big sign. What's more, it had to be fixed on the external wall between the third and six floors. I asked the hoist driver to lift the sign and attach the upper angle bars to the roof, and I myself climbed out from a window on the third floor, and then stood on the angle bars and drilled, without any safety harness. To tell you the truth, I was scared. But who else would do the job if I didn't? When I was drilling the holes outside the sixth floor, I looked down and felt dizzy. I tried to control my fear and concentrate on my work without looking down and thinking about the danger. Once the installation was finished, I looked at the big sign hung on the building and felt proud of myself. It showed that nothing was impossible!

In the evening as I went home by motorbike, running through busy traffic and dazzling neon signs, I saw the neon signs that I had made and installed, and I couldn't help slowing down and admiring them.

From working for others to running my own business, I have gradually come to understand the ways of the world and human relationships. My own character has changed, from being simple and honest to being tactful and articulate. As I have come to realize, anyone can change. When I am in a discussion with the clients, I need to figure out their thoughts while remaining calm and clear-headed myself. Any mistake I make could ruin my business. For this reason, I am always conscious of the value of wit and eloquence, and try to improve myself through practice.

My ambitions are to make breakthroughs in the design of neon signs and make better products than my competitors. When I have enough money, I will open my own advertising company.

I Have Never Been Homesick

Narrator: Zhang Sheng, male, 20, from Qingxiu District of Nanning City, Guangxi Zhuang Autonomous Region
Job: hotel attendant – warehouse inspector – supervisor of leather bag processing
Work place: Dongguan, Guangdong Province

I should thank the mountains of Guangxi. They nurtured me and the pine trees on these mountains became the source of my first "pot of gold." The lumber business is the main channel for local people to make money. In small towns there are transfer stations, and lumber is transported down from the mountains to first one and then another town. The stations charge differently. I worked for my uncle as an agent, making around 100 yuan per day dealing with the transfer stations. I was happy with such a life. But I was also saddened by the sight of the disappearing forests.

Gradually, I found the work too tiring as I had to travel into the mountains by truck almost every day. I started to think: when will I get out of mountains? And then an accident occurred and I made up my mind to leave.

A Qiang, the youngest worker, was a college graduate, majoring in landscape engineering. He said that finding a job had been more difficult than finding a wife. He could not find suitable work and had to stay in the mountains and deal in lumber. One day a big tree fell down on him and we saw him die. After the funeral, I told my family members without hesitation, "I have to leave!"

Carrying my luggage, I went to Dongguan by myself.

Hotel Attendant

Processing, manufacturing, service…. The human resource market covered different fields. I tried to find a job here, among numerous job-hunters. Seeing university graduates also looking for jobs, I was discouraged, but when I saw middle-aged men, I felt confident, since being young I had an advantage over them. I forget how many application forms I filled in that first day. I was on the point of leaving, but a five-star hotel showed interest, and I went into the interview room without hesitation. Five department managers read my resume and asked me again and again the same routine questions. Their interviews irritated me; moreover, I was afraid of being caught out in that some parts of my resume were fake. When they finally decided to hire me, I felt like the luckiest man in the world.

Later when I got to know my department manager better, I asked her light-heartedly why they had chosen me. She smiled and said, "Because you look simple in appearance but are crafty…." I was surprised. You have to be cunning to survive. And what looked to them like slyness would be admired as "brightness" in my hometown. But I persisted, and joked, "Were you aware that a lot of my resume was fake?" She patted me on the shoulder and laughed, "How many job-hunters are going to stick to the truth nowadays?" My eyes were opened to a new truth: some people habitually lie, and some are willing to be deceived.

The job was easy to learn. Most of the time I only needed to do as the others were doing. And I could earn more than 1,000 yuan per month. The wage was not as high as in my former job, but this bustling city was quite different from the out-of-the-way countryside. I had a strong sense that I was breathing the same air that rich people breathed.

Many of the customers at our hotel were rich: they used imported perfume, wore brand necklaces, drove brand sports cars, and even walked in a different manner. In a phrase, they were filthy rich…. There was a time when I was eager to become one of them…. But the reality was I had to humble myself in their presence. I learned how to be worldly-wise and how to get along with people.

A Bankrupt Factory

When I grew weary of this job, I turned to factory work. Within a year, I would witness the downfall of one of the top 100 enterprises in China.

My job was on a production line. The wage was a bit higher than that of hotel attendant, but the workload was unexpectedly heavy. Every day I was on my feet for more than 10 hours; when we had to work shifts, our endurance would be tested to the limits. It was probably through tiredness that mistakes occurred. Truckloads of goods were returned, usually because the trademark or code bar had been put in the wrong place. When we worked together and completed an order, we felt a sense of accomplishment. When we had to offload goods from trucks, we felt downcast – it meant we would have to spend another day correcting mistakes that we should have avoided. Of course, we would complain; the punishment was not serious, but anyone who had made the mistakes would feel bad.

Soon the manager found out I was careful, and let me be an

inspector. I was happy with the change as I no longer needed to work beside the clattering machinery. I applied myself to my work with enthusiasm, and often noticed errors that had been missed by others. As a result of my hard work, the manager thought highly of me. But my wage was reflected by my workload, and I still had to work day and night.

Going home for Spring Festival had advantages and disadvantages. I was glad to be going back to the place where I had grown up. But I felt down because I had not won fame or fortune, despite the time I had spent working elsewhere.

I took comfort in the fact that I was a good worker, and I got on with my job without letting myself be distracted. But who could have guessed that the company president was involved in wrongdoing? The case caused a sensation, and I started to fear for the factory. Everyone became jittery; workers would pause at their jobs to watch these men in uniform going in and out. Soon the factory gate was sealed with paper strips, and we workers had to find other employment.... While I was resting at home, I got a call from my manager, who thought highly of me. He told me that even though the president had been imprisoned, there were still a lot of semi-finished products to be processed; although the factory's reputation and profits had suffered he hoped I would think it over and go back to work.

But I did not return. I heard that after struggling on for a while, the factory eventually went bankrupt.

My Life as a Supervisor

Later I heard that a distant relative had opened a foreign trade company in Dongguan. He was married to a local woman and had a foreign-style house and a car.... I admired him and went to him for help. Of course, I was not so naive as to go to work for him. I thought that he would assume that I was used to hard days, and pay me a low wage. Instead, I talked him into introducing me to another foreign trade company.

It was a bag manufacturing company. This job was the easiest one I had ever seen: I did not need to beat my brains out or use my hands. As a supervisor, I only needed to cooperate with other supervisors and oversee workers to ensure that they did not turn out substandard goods. At first, I was astonished by the simplicity of the work, and even thought of helping out with the work myself. But I didn't want to be seen as a workaholic, so I didn't pursue the idea. I was strict with workers, and they often said I was working them too hard. I replied with a smile, "These bags are to be sold overseas. How could I give foreigners any opportunity to belittle our Chinese craftsmanship?"

The conditions I enjoyed were much better than before. A spacious room, wood floor, wall-mounted air-conditioner.... Every room was equipped with all mod-cons, apart from a computer. I think foreign-funded enterprises are far better than our state-owned enterprises in this regard. Sometimes when I saw people working hard, I understood the approach of those foreign CEOs. They respected each other, and high-level managers would not hang around if nothing special was going on. The atmosphere here was far better than any of the other places where I had worked. I admired their business sense, which I thought might be one of the factors behind the gap between them and us.

Once I had got to know our company's engineer, he put together a computer for me. I was grateful to him, and envied him his skills, since such a simple thing in his eyes was something I could never have done on my own. I began to develop a deep respect for such "knowledge" and believed it must have considerable merit.

At this foreign trade company, I often encountered foreigners, black and white. Many workers respected them, and kept their distance. But I often greeted them. I found them friendly, and they would often give a thumbs-up to show approval of the workers' attitude. Unfortunately, I could only smile and say "hello" or "hi," which embarrassed me a lot.

The company had many university graduates of about the same age as me. Although I was paid a similar salary, I resented their condescending manner toward me. Although I had many years of work experience, there were occasions when they were my superiors. When they were engaged in debating some issue, for example, I could only sneak off in silence. I found this very embarrassing. I was frustrated by the way they would show off their talents, but I did not know what to do. On the one hand, I would tell myself that it was beneath me to get involved in their showing-off, but at the same time I couldn't help admiring the life of intellectuals. I started to understand that education could make a difference to a person, and that knowledge could put on show.... Many of my friends who were still at college or university complained to me: study was tiring; they were in debt as they had to spend their parents' money; they wanted to earn a living like me. I told them with a smile, "You are earning money too. For the time being it's still an intangible asset. You will know its value when you reap it." I often thought it ridiculous that these people did not appreciate the happy life they were enjoying.

Many people look down on our migrant workers. But society is a big family. If I do not adapt myself to it, I will never be accepted. I think the best thing I can do is to keep away from bad things. I have been away from home for several years, but I have never been homesick. It is strange. Perhaps it is because I know I still have a long road to travel before going home....

Can I Ever Go Back to My Studies?

Narrator: Tao Fang, female, 20, from Qichun County of Huanggang City, Hubei Province
Job: worker in a flax mill – waitress – worker in a clothing factory
Work place: in town – Shanghai – Shenzhen, Guangdong Province

My family lived in a small town. We rented a small run-down bungalow, which stood out among the surrounding two-storied buildings. When I was young, my family was not wealthy but life was OK and the four family members were healthy. During the 1990s there were several prosperous factories in my town, and most locals worked in these factories and lived off their wages. Older people say the workers were well-off at the time. My dad worked at one of the factories, and his monthly wage was 400-500 yuan, a substantial amount in those days. My mom worked from home making shoes and clothes for others to help out with the family expenses, and during the Spring Festival she sold leaf tea. The money they earned mostly went to pay for my own and my younger sister's schooling, so our life was frugal. Sometimes Dad joked, "If you and your sister didn't go to school, our family would live a more comfortable life." But I knew Dad did not really mean that. One of our neighbors had supported two children who had completed university education, and they enjoyed a well-paid urban life. How could Dad not envy them? How could he not hope to support my sister and me until we got to university? He knew that education was an intangible asset. As a parent, he had not had the chance to get hold of this asset, but he could provide it to his children.

But Dad failed to realize his dream. For all his determination, he could do nothing.

One year, he contracted hepatitis B and was subsequently laid off. I was only 13 years old, in the second year of junior high school. My younger sister was three years younger, in the fifth grade of primary school. Our tuition and fees totaled 500-600 yuan per semester, a heavy burden for a family with an unemployed father. At that time, I was too young to understand my hardworking parents, or help with the housework, or care for my Dad, as I had no real idea of what hepatitis B entailed. The only thing I was concerned with was whether I would have to leave school. But my worries were unfounded. Dad and Mom insisted on supporting us through school, even though it was difficult for our family. They never talked about how hard up they were in our presence. Our life went on as usual.

Although Dad was sick, he was even busier than before. He had been an electrician and technician responsible for machine maintenance at the factory. After leaving the factory, he did whatever work he could find, not taking care of himself properly. At that time, I could not understand why I could not see Dad before bedtime, and why he did not care about my studies or help me with my homework. What was even more frustrating was that Dad said nothing to encourage me when I finished in top 10 during the mid-term exam. I thought Dad didn't really want me to go to school, and thus I did not study as hard as before. One day, when I came home after school, I smelled a strong odor of traditional Chinese herbs. It turned out that Dad's illness had worsened due to his tiredness, and Mom was preparing a decoction for him. From then on, Dad was "idle" while the bitter smell of Chinese herbs lingered on in our house and gradually became part of our life. Almost every day Mom would pour the black sediment on the path in front of our house. Mom said passers-by could take away Dad's disease by walking through the sediment. I did not think so, and murmured to myself: Superstition.... But for all that I knew it was impossible, part of me went on hoping that passers-by could take Dad's illness with them. Mom might also have known it was impossible, but she carried on with the ritual day after day, praying for Dad's recovery....

Leaving School

As time passed, Dad's health deteriorated and he had to take more medicine. The smell of herbal concoctions grew stronger and stronger, and we grew more worried and upset. The shortage of money for Dad's treatment and our tuition fees cast a shadow over our home, and I started to think about leaving school.

In 2002, I was enrolled into a senior high school in our town. I knew this would place my parents in a dilemma and make our financial situation even worse. In the meantime, Dad's hepatitis worsened and he developed liver ascites as he had not had proper treatment over a protracted period. His abdomen grew swollen, his complexion turned darker and darker, and he lost vitality. At its worst, Dad could drink or eat nothing, and had to depend on a nutrient injection every day to keep him going. But a nutrient injection cost more than 300 yuan, and consequently our family ran into debt – a lot of money. Mom was so worried that she could not sleep for days, and I was often woken in the night by her weeping.

Finally, I had to quit school. Although Dad was reluctant, it was the only option. I did not complain, but swore an oath to myself: from then on, I would work hard and earn money to pay for my Dad's treatment, improve our financial situation, and support my younger sister though university in place of my own dream.

Temporary Worker in a Flax mill

That year, I was 15 years old, and one of my relatives found me a job in a flax mill as a temporary worker. My work was to sort the flax and pack it. At first, I had no experience and was often criticized by my team leader, who said I was too slow and inefficient. To catch up with others, I trained hard. Gradually, I adapted myself to the work. I did well, and sometimes completed my work ahead of time. Thus I earned a year-end bonus. But the work was dirty and tiring, and the eight-hour day was too heavy for an adolescent. I fainted twice in the workshop as a result of physical exhaustion, congenital anemia, and malnutrition. The dust from the mill gave me frequent coughs. And my tender hands were covered with hard calluses.

After a day's work, I was usually covered with flax dust, like a figure buried underground for years. What was worse, the flax was so light that it could stick to any part of my body, and get into my nose, ears and throat. But I was willing to work there for the monthly wage of 500 yuan, plus the year-end bonus and the household articles we were offered on holidays. And my wage certainly helped reduce the burden on our family.

Every day, I would rush home after work on an old bicycle that used to belong to my Dad. I knew that Dad would be waiting for me at home with a tasty meal. Although he was sick, he would not lie around like a disabled person. When he felt better, he raised chickens and ducks and planted vegetables in our backyard, to save on living costs and earn a little additional money. When I got home, tired, Dad would often look at me with affection and sometimes heave a sigh.

Although he said nothing, I knew he felt guilty at being unable to support my education or help me with my hard work. The only thing he could do was to prepare good meals for me. Sometime, I did feel tired at work. But when I thought that I was carrying my share of the family's burden, I did not complain to my parents. The poor man's child shares the household burden. I had a thorough understanding of this saying.

Saying Goodbye to My Schooldays

After leaving school, I spent almost all my time in tiring and boring work. Even when I had time for any leisure, I stayed at home and had a good sleep or watched TV, as I could not afford to take a vacation. My life seemed empty of any pleasure. I recalled my schooldays. Although study was intense, I still tried to find time to read books and periodicals, to widen my knowledge and broaden my horizons. But after leaving school, I became estranged from reading. Even if I had time and energy, I could not apply myself to reading. My daily routine led from home to mill and home again. I felt very isolated from the outside world.

When I recalled my schooldays, I would feel unhappy. At school, I was single-minded, and thought of nothing but study. In class, I concentrated on acquiring knowledge; after class I could play with classmates. But after leaving school, everything changed. Due to the pressures I was under, I lost self-confidence. Perhaps it was because of the sudden change in lifestyle that I could no longer find anything worth chatting about. The only pastime I had was standing alongside my workmates (mostly married) listening to them talking about trivial household matters and gossiping about neighbors. But this held no interest for me.

I still kept in contact with former classmates and sometimes visited them. Sadly, I found that we had less and less in common, and I was often unable to join in their conversations. Then I would feel a sense of inferiority. Once, I went window-shopping with two former classmates who were studying at a senior high school. At first, they were curious about my work, and I told them how I felt about it. Then they talked about fresh news of their school and classes, and I, having been cut off from education, could play no part in their conversation. They then suggested we go to an Internet café. At that time the Internet was still a new thing for most people. There were only a few cafés in our town, and the customers were mainly fashionable senior high school students. I knew nothing about the Internet, and declined the offer with the excuse that I had to get to work. The truth was that I did not dare to go to the café because I was afraid that I would lose face and they would laugh at me. This caused me considerable distress. Gradually, I lost courage and confidence and my contact with these former friends came to an end.

Working at a Korean Restaurant in Shanghai

I worked at the mill for nearly two years and learned the ways of the world. However, as more and more people left to go further afield, and the town's economy slowed down, the mill saw its profits dropping and had to downsize its staff. Sometimes it could not pay workers on time. Forced to look for another job, I became one of the numerous migrant workers. People said it was easier to earn money outside our town, and there was gold to be mined elsewhere. Being young, I was tempted by the dazzle of the outside world, and decided to go out and seek my fortune.

In 2004, I was 16 years old. An agent brought me and other children of my age to Shanghai where I had dreamed of living. It was really another world altogether.

I worked at a Korean restaurant in Pudong, Shanghai's most bustling district. I worked from 8:00 to 12:00, from 14:00 to 17:00 and from 19:00 to 21:00. My wage was 800 yuan a month, and the restaurant provided board and lodging. As it was a Korean restaurant, most of the customers were foreigners. Thus one rule of the restaurant was that all staff must speak basic everyday Korean. At first, I could not speak any Korean and knew nothing about the catering industry, and thus could only do simple labor, like cleaning and dishwashing, which left me aching all over. At times like this I would feel homesick. At least at home Dad would care for me. But here I had to put up with all this by myself. In my free time I went out with girls from our town and strolled around. But everything was so expensive that I could only go window-shopping. I sometimes saw the others looking at me with disdain.

After a short while, I began to pick up some basic knowledge of etiquette and a little simple Korean, and I started to work as a waitress, accepting orders and serving customers. I came to like the work — the restaurant was a good one, I was learning a foreign language, and I was gaining useful experience. But one day, an event occurred that tempered my enthusiasm and wounded my pride.

Wishing to Get Back to School

That day, two foreigners (non-Koreans) came into the restaurant and spoke to me in a stream of English that was so quick that I could not understand. I was only a middle school graduate. I shook my head in anxiety. Seeing my embarrassment, they stole a glance at each other and grinned. I turned to my head waitress for help. That moment stirred up feelings within me. I cursed my ignorance, and the idea of going home and back to school entered my mind. But the prospect seemed faint to me, a person who had missed her chance of and access to education. As a country girl, how could I secure for myself another chance of education and campus life? I had to keep this aspiration buried deep in heart....

At the end of the year, I got my annual salary from the boss. The boss only paid us 300 yuan for living expenses from the 800-yuan monthly wage, withholding the rest till the year end. He said in this way, we would not waste our money. But in fact, he kept the rest of our wages back to make sure we didn't quit half way through the year. If anyone quit, the boss would simply keep their money. Eager to get home, I boarded a train to my hometown. Before coming to Shanghai I had been desperate to experience life here. But now, my outlook was rather more sophisticated. During my days in Shanghai, I had become aware of the insurmountable gap between urban and rural people and had gone through embarrassment, humiliation and shame – all this because I was a migrant worker and a rural resident, not an urban one, like Shanghainese. They could find all sorts of ways to humiliate me, all sorts of ways to remind me: you are a villager! All sorts of these minor details hurt my pride. Sometimes I would ask myself: could knowledge build a protective wall around my self-esteem? Would education alter the urban residents' harsh attitude toward a rural resident? But where was my education? Would I still have the right to education, and the opportunity to secure that right?

All of My Family Becoming Migrant Workers

Sometimes I felt like a wounded animal, eager to get back to my snug and familiar home, lick my wounds, and recover.

Back in my familiar hometown, I found everything agreeable.

Dad looked no different, suffering from occasional relapses. Mom looked older from the years she had spent rushing around seeking medical help for Dad's disease. My younger sister had become sensible and considerate, but she wanted to leave school and go to work, as I had done. Perhaps she wanted to relieve the burden on our family, or escape the boredom of her schooldays, or get out and see the wonders of the outside world as I had done. Whatever her reasons, I resolutely opposed the idea. And I recounted my bitter experiences to her, trying to convince her that the outside world was not as exciting as it seemed, and that I had to endure loneliness and sarcasm on my own. I told her that only with a good education could she avoid mockery, and look forward to the prospect of a happy life; without education, she would know suffering. On every occasion that I sat earnestly trying to make my sister see sense, Dad sat beside us, his head bowed, sighing in distress. Although he did not want me to see it or know it, I knew he was still blaming himself for the ending of my education. However, my sister insisted, against all our advice, while for my part I dared not voice the secret wish of going back to school that lay deep in my heart…. I knew that I had long since lost the chance.

At the beginning of 2005, Dad's illness resulted in a lot of expense. As a result, Mom had to go to Hunan to work in a shoemaking factory. I decided not to go back to Shanghai, but went to Dongguan to work in a clothing factory, while my sister went to a factory in Shenzhen. Dad stayed at home; our old grandma would take care of him. No one wanted to see our close family falling apart, particularly Dad. When he saw us off, he looked rueful and helpless. He felt anxious and guilty for becoming a burden on us. The distress caused by our departures quickly resulted in a turn for the worse.

Painful Farewell

In the summer of 2006, Dad's disease reached an advanced stage.

The family went home and stayed with him for a month. During that month, Dad took a turn for the better, perhaps because of the family bonds. But our respective employers urged us to get back to work, and we had to do so. This time, we parted from Dad for ever. Toward the end of the year, Mom called me one day in tears, saying that Dad was dying and asking me to go home. I did not have time to react to the sudden news, or to sorrow and weep. Three days later, I got home, but Dad could no longer see me or speak. My sister got home a day later as a result of a delay in getting money from her boss. That day, Mom prepared dumplings, and asked us not to cry in front of Dad. We nodded through our tears....

At noon, all of our family ate dumplings together, and Dad closed his eyes and passed quietly away....

Now I often regret that I did not continue my education; the poverty that impelled me resulted in lifelong heartache both for me and for my Dad.

Dad, if there is an afterlife I promise that I will go to school there, and make amends for your lifetime of unfulfilled dreams.

Working around China

Narrator: Zhao Fangshuan, male, 23, from Zhaoxin Village in Hengshui City, Hebei Province
Job: road roller driver – maintenance personnel – wedding cameraman – road worker
Work place: Beijing – Dongguan, Guangdong Province – Hangzhou, Zhejiang Province – Shuozhou, Shanxi Province – Hengshui, Hebei Province

When I was young, I knew nothing but play. I did not study hard at middle school and as a consequence my results were poor. After the Spring Festival in 2000, two months before the senior high school entrance exam, I needed to pay the school 60 yuan as an exam fee and more than 300 yuan in tuition fees. At that time, my elder brother was getting married, and our family was short of money. Mom asked me, "Do you really think you will pass this exam?" I didn't answer, nor did I ask for money again. That meant giving up the chance to take the exam. To tell the truth, I felt sad at the time.

Driving a Roller at the Age of 16

One of my Dad's friends helped me find a job as a road roller driver on a road-building site. During the working day we were provided with five meals at 8:00, 11:00, 14:00, 18:00 and midnight. Later I was on night shift and went home by bike at noon.

When paving a road, workers would spread lime on the ground, leaving a soft surface. One time a villager drove a tractor onto the new road surface. The tractor got stuck and sank even deeper when the villager tried to rev the engine. When he saw me driving my roller nearby, he asked me to help him, and I agreed. The 18-ton roller pulled the tractor out of the lime. The villager thanked me again and again.

When I returned to the site, colleagues came up and asked me, "How much did you charge him?"

"Nothing," I answered.

"You didn't charge him! Did you ask for cigarettes?"

"I don't smoke, so I didn't ask for any."

"You did it for nothing? You're stupid!"

I felt puzzled: I had helped the villager. I had done a good deed. Why were these people criticizing me? Do we need to ask for something in return for helping others? Only 16, I did not know what to do.

I once came off duty after 19:00 with several workmates. We saw a small white truck leave the road and fall into a trench, knocking down two young trees. My workmates said, "Let's go and have a look. We can help pull the truck out and maybe get some money for wine." Under the dim streetlights we saw two men getting out of the truck and talking. Maybe they were discussing whether to call someone to help them pull out the truck. We came up and said that we could pull out the truck for 100 yuan. They said they had no money and did not need our help. One of my workmates threatened them, "If you don't let us pull out the truck, I will report you to the highway bureau for knocking down the trees – 800 yuan for each!" So saying, he made as if to head off on his motorbike. The driver immediately stopped him, saying "Don't do that, pal. We'll let you help us. OK?" The two sides agreed on the terms and I went to fetch the roller. Some of my workmates tied a wire cable between the truck and roller, while others watched for passing vehicles. We soon pulled the truck out. But the two men went back on their word and refused to pay us the 100 yuan. We said, "We put a lot of work into this. You could at least buy us a meal." The driver said he did not have enough money. One of my workmates took the tarpaulin off the truck. The driver begged us, "Don't take our tarpaulin. We still need it." Another workmate from Shandong said, "Get real! We gave you a lot of help. The least you could do is buy us some beer on such a hot day. Are you going to give us something or not? Otherwise, we're keeping the tarpaulin." We argued for some time, and finally went back to the construction site with the tarpaulin.

I worked there for more than four months, and earned over 2,000 yuan.

Studying Maintenance at School

Then I wanted to acquire some home appliance maintenance skills to earn a living. One of my neighbors told me that Oriental Technical School of Hengshui City was not bad, charging 800 yuan for a semester. So I went to study there, and stayed in the house of one of my sisters, not far from the school. At the end of the first month, I felt very homesick – it was the first time I had lived away from home.

Once, my sister had a problem with her color TV. I told her that

I would take it to school to mend it. For more than a week, I tried to repair it, and finally thought I had found the problem. I bought a new part and changed it, but it turned out I was wrong. I then turned to a teacher for help. He checked the TV and said the problem was coming from the power-supply unit. I changed the part and suddenly the image on the screen was back. I was filled with admiration for the teacher, and became more determined to master these skills.

In the spring of 2001, I was due to graduate. The headmaster asked me whether I would be looking for an internship or a job. I had heard that the job would be installing air-conditioners in shopping malls, and that it was heavy work. So I decided to opt for an internship. He arranged for me to go to Beijing, where the employer would provide board and lodging. With five other schoolmates I started off on the journey, carrying my luggage and my diploma.

We were told to wait at the station, as the employer would send a vehicle to take us to the workplace. But after we arrived, we waited for more than an hour and nobody showed up. Finally two men came to welcome us, saying "Load your luggage onto our vehicle." When they showed us the vehicle, we didn't know whether to laugh or cry. It was a bike. The two men had come to fetch the six of us by bike!

Carrying our beddings and possessions, we walked for about half an hour through streets and lanes, and finally got to a home appliance maintenance store called Jubaolong Service Center. It comprised a shop front and two other rooms – a workshop and a dormitory. We put down our luggage and had a look at the workshop. It was only 20 sq m. There was some machinery and some equipment for repairing home appliances, and several big mirrors on the wall used to check the image of TV sets.

In the evening, we had dinner: one dish and one soup, both

made of bean sprouts, and steamed buns. The dormitory was even worse. The small room was crowded with bunk beds for more than 20 people. But I told myself: I've come here to work as an intern; the conditions don't matter. The important thing is to add to my skills. I did not get any of the beds, so I used two cardboard boxes from TV sets as my bed. But during the night I woke up full of aches and pains. The boxes had collapsed and I had fallen onto the ground. And that's where I ended up sleeping. The following morning, the boss gathered us together and talked about our internship: it would be three months; those who performed well could stay on and get a monthly salary of more than 1,000 yuan. But we would have to buy our own tools and bikes.

Four Internship Days in Beijing

We were annoyed by this news of the tools. The school had told us not to bring tools with us, and now it turned out that in fact we did need them. But the first problem to be solved was a bike, otherwise we couldn't get around. Another intern and I each contributed 25 yuan, and we bought a second-hand bike. Then I went out to work with a senior worker. I was feeling hungry and said, "Mr Xu, let's buy something to eat." "OK," he said. "You pay for yourself and I'll pay for myself." I had never expected him to pay for me! He judged the heart of another man by his own mean standards! I bought two cakes and ate them while we walked.

We arrived at a customer's house. When the TV set was turned on, the screen was dark, with a bright line in the middle. The client asked whether something was wrong with the tube. I had dealt with this problem on many occasions, and knew where it came from, but I wanted to see what Mr Xu would do. To my surprise, he told the client that the circuit board in the cabinet was broken and the repair would cost 90 yuan. The client tried to bargain. But Xu said, "That's our bottom price. We work for our employer. The store has rules. We cannot make it less." So the client agreed and we started to repair the TV set. Xu welded a broken line on the circuit board with a soldering iron. Thus he got his 90 yuan without even changing any parts. Happily, he pocketed the money. By the time we finished, it was after 11 o'clock. I looked at him and he said, "Look, I earned the money. I'm not giving you any. Once you're a skilled technician, you'll get your turn." "I understand," I replied. "Shall we go back to the store for lunch?" He grinned and said, "Go, if you want. You'll find steamed buns and bean sprouts if you can get back before 12 o'clock."

After lunch we hurried on our way without a break. After some effort, we finally found our second customer. The customer had called the store, wanting to have a circuit board repaired. But when we found the client it turned out to be an appliance maintenance shop. Mr Xu checked the circuit board and gave a price of 130 yuan for taking it back to our store and repairing it. The shop owner contacted the customer and told him that professionals from a brand-name maintenance center would have to repair the board and the fee would be 160 yuan. The customer agreed, and we took back the circuit board. I thought to myself: these people really know how to do business. They gave the laymen a higher price and the difference was 30 yuan.

Then we went on to our third customer. It was already dark. This client's TV set was still under warranty. According to the rules of our store, he should not have had to pay any maintenance charge. But Mr Xu still charged 30 yuan after repairing it in no more than 20 minutes. The client asked Xu to repair a set of stereo equipment, and Xu worked on it for about half an hour, then said he would come back to finish it. The customer asked whether he could use a broken VCR to pay for the job, and Xu was happy to agree. By the time we left this customer's house, it was already past 8 o'clock. I was tired and rode slowly under the dim street lights. Xu told me, "Don't tell the boss how much we made today. The repairs we did weren't easy, and I have to work hard to support my family. And we rode more than 100 *li* today." Back at the center, I found myself eating steamed buns and bean sprouts yet again.

This was the first day of my internship. I was aching all over, but I had picked up some useful experience, and felt that it was well worth it.

But we interns could not put up with such a life. On the fourth day, two schoolmates and I decided to quit. The boss told us dismissively, "Go now, and that will be the end of your prospects in this trade." I wasn't convinced. "I don't believe you! I'll make something of myself." Then we three packed up and returned home. Our four-day internship in Beijing was over.

After getting back home, I put together a soldering iron, a multimeter, a screwdriver and some other basic maintenance tools, and opened a small home appliance maintenance store in my house. I repaired washing machines, TV sets, VCRs, and a few other common household appliances. At first, business was slow. That winter I moved the store to one of the country markets, serving the surrounding villages, and business picked up. I regularly read the textbooks from the technical school while putting the theory into practice, and it soon became clear to me that the knowledge that I had acquired at school was superficial and far from sufficient for my practical needs.

Wedding Cameraman

After the Spring Festival in 2003, I bought a video recorder for more than 4,000 yuan. I went out to take videos in the busy season (in November and December), and went back to run the store in the remaining months of the year.

In the spring of 2004, I closed down my small home appliance maintenance store. I was starting to feel rather weary of the work after spending so long in this field of business. Then I got involved in wedding photography, and preparing opening ceremonies for clients.

I often encountered malfunctions and technical problems. It was especially cold in the winter of 2004. Once, at about 4:00 in the morning, I was on my way to videotape a wedding. As I prepared to start work, the screen of my recorder showed "E07," a sign of malfunction. I immediately broke out in a cold sweat, and asked myself, "What am I going to do?" The bridegroom kindly told me not to worry. "But something's wrong," I said. "And I'm not going to be able to record your wedding." I made a few calls for help. But it was too early, and no one answered. Fortunately, after about two minutes, the screen cleared and the machine returned to normal, so I was able to work on and record the wedding successfully. Later, a senior cameraman from the shop where I had bought the recorder told me that when it was cold or wet, dew could form on the magnetic drum, but the machine would return to normal once it had been on for a few minutes. So it was a false alarm. But it showed that I lacked experience and knowledge. Later, when I encountered similar difficulties, I would tell myself: this is just the darkness before dawn – the first light of morning will soon appear.

I had another example. On one occasion, the battery charge showing on the screen didn't look right. When I tried to record there wasn't enough power. I found a storage battery from a motorbike and two wires. Before I connected the battery to the recorder, the indicator light of the recorder was on; but after I connected them, the light went off. Whatever I tried, it stayed off. The recorder was still under warranty, so I called the shop and said that I was bringing the recorder to them. It was already past 22:00. I rode to the city center of Hengshui. The workers there checked the recorder but could not find the cause of the problem. They asked me to return the recorder to the manufacturer. I said, "I don't have time, I have a job tomorrow." So I decided to take the recorder back home and repair it myself. It was after midnight by the time I got home.

I got up before six in the morning. I took the recorder apart with the tools I had used to do my home appliance repairs. I was immediately stunned. All the parts were as small as those in a mobile phone. What could I do? I had nobody to help me. I just had to try whatever I could. I used my multimeter to test the parts. I spotted some electric resistors wrapped in white coils, and thought they must have some special function. When I tested them I got a bigger reading from one of them than the others, and I realized it was a safety resistor. I tested it several times, and confirmed that this was the only one that was different. I guessed something was wrong with this resistor. By then the bridegroom had already called me several times. I answered, and then carried on with my repair work. I did not have much time. So I decided to treat the resistor as if it was a fuse. I bypassed the resistor with some fine steel wire, which I soldered around the resistor. I knew if I was wrong, the recorder would never work. The risk was that by adding another fuse, the electric current would increase and burn out the recorder's motor. But I had no choice. Once the soldering was complete I checked the parts several times, connected the recorder to the power supply, and turned it on. The indicator light turned on, and everything was normal. I breathed a hearty sigh of relief. Although it had taken me less than two hours, it felt an awful lot longer. Having succeeded in repairing the camera, I was able to record the wedding. Whenever I recalled that case, it would send a shiver down my spine. As the saying goes, I dug myself out of a deep hole.

The wedding work was not regular, so my income was not stable. Sometimes I went elsewhere to work as a temporary roadman. It was harder work, but the money was better and I could broaden my horizons by visiting new places.

Southward: 25 Days in Dongguan

There was a factory producing expansion joints in our neighboring village. A friend helped me find work there. Expansion joints are also called temperature joints, and they are used on roads to adjust for temperature changes. Temperature changes will result in expansion or contraction of construction materials and other parts, and consequently long roads will split or even break. Therefore, long roads are often divided into sections with expansion joints between the sections, so that each section can expand or contract independently and the roads will not split or break.

A salesman from the factory won a contract to install expansion joints on a project in Guangdong, and I was one of those given the job. The employer would pay traveling expenses and provide board and lodging. I was so excited that I could hardly sleep. I was going out to gain some experience.

In April 2004, I boarded a train for the south with the salesman, my elder cousin and seven others. After 25 hours, we arrived at Dongguan Railway Station. It was already past midnight so we stayed in a station waiting room until dawn.

The next day, we went to Dalingshan Town, a small place with beautiful scenery, high buildings and busy traffic. Soon, the expansion joints were shipped to the construction site. We set to work immediately, installing them on a two-way four-lane road numbered Section 5, and a bridge numbered Section 9.

I was assigned to work on Section 5 with three other men. The salesman took on the task of labor contractor and supervisor. Four days later, a middle-aged man wearing glasses told us to stop work. He said our work did not meet the specification and we would have to disassemble all the joints. Later we learned that the salesman had got the Section 5 contract through bribery, but other bidders were unwilling to give up on the job and had managed to get it back. We workers had nothing to do with any of this, but we had to disassemble all the expansion joints that we had assembled. We had sealed the joints on the two right lanes with cement and there was no way to disassemble them; we had only welded the two left lanes, so we could dismantle them with cutting torches. Although it was April, it was hot in Dongguan. The work kept us in a constant sweat, so we constantly washed our heads and faces with cold water, which we also drank. Perhaps we were not accustomed to the climate there, and three of us ended up with sickness and diarrhea, but we had to carry on with the work. We spent two days clearing Section 5, then went to work on Section 9.

While working on Section 9, my cousin and I were on the lowest rate, 50 yuan per day, while our workmates, having some additional skills, got 10 yuan more than us. On the third morning, four of us had breakfast at a roadside stall, buying 20 steamed stuffed buns. We ate fast, and swallowed one bun in three or four bites. The locals stared at us, so much so that we were embarrassed. It turned out that we northerners ate more than southerners. One bun was enough for a southern worker in the morning, while we each had five. That was what had amazed them so.

One night, we found our contractor grinning from ear to ear. We were puzzled. Why was he looking so pleased with himself? He told us that our expansion joints had gone missing. Now we were even more puzzled. He explained with a smile, "Our expansion joints were put into a warehouse as soon as they were brought here, and I got a receipt. That meant the joints were under the care of the warehouse, and no longer our responsibility. Now that they are gone, the manager here says he will pay compensation for all the lost joints. And I can tell him whatever amount I want! No wonder I'm so happy!"

At the end of the job, we had to hurry on and work day and night. On the last day, the date of our return tickets, my cousin and I had to do rounding-off work. At about 11 o'clock in the morning, we both finished our work and went back to the site for our pay. It should have been 1,250 yuan for 25 days. But the contractor found some fault with my work and deducted more than 100 yuan. Then it was another 25 hours on the train home.

Eastward: 23 Days in Hangzhou

In late August 2004, a contractor from Xiaohou Village was recruiting workers in neighboring villages to install expansion joints near Hangzhou, Zhejiang Province.

The section where we were going to work was in the mountains on the Ningbo-Jinhua Expressway. As soon as we arrived, we were sent to check our sections and did not even have time to set up our cabins. Each person was responsible for one part of the section, making sure that no vehicles ran over the fresh cement of the expansion joints. I found a place by the side of the road, spread out my quilt, and lay down. But I slept badly, constantly waking up. By midnight my quilt was so soaked with dew that I could wring the water out of it. But I had to get some sleep. I spent a fearful night tossing and turning by the side of the road. In the morning, I watched the sunrise. It was the first time I had seen a sunrise in the mountains. It was gorgeous! Armed with this experience, I would be able to show off when I got home. I was bold! I had slept all night, alone by the side of an expressway! Aha!

After two days looking after the road, our cabins were set up. Back at the construction site, the work was divided up. I and three other men were assigned to go on the night shift. In south China, when it starts to rain it usually carries on raining. During the time we spent there, the weather was not good. But we still had to work all night, a piece of plastic sheeting draped over our shoulders. Sometimes, I suffered from the shakes due to the endless rain. One night, it was raining and I got the shakes. While trying to cut openings on the asphalt road with a hammer and a metal chisel, I hit so hard that the punch flew to the side and hit my left ankle. At first my left foot went numb; then I felt a severe pain. I was sent to a clinic, where the doctor said it was only a bruise and then bandaged up my ankle. But I was still in considerable pain. I only took one day of rest and then went back to work, even though my ankle was swollen and I was limping. Nobody cared about me. I just had to put up with the pain by myself. Sometimes the mental pain was even harder to bear. I was far from home and missed home very much. When my mother sometimes called me, I only ever told her good news and would say, "I'm fine. Don't worry. Don't call me if there's no news. Telephone calls are expensive."

Westward: 17 Days in Shuozhou

In September 2006, a friend from a neighboring village and I went to Shuozhou in Shanxi Province on a truck loaded with expansion joints. We passed through Niangzi and Yanmen, two majestic passes on the Great Wall. Driving on the mountain roads was an adventure. When climbing up a hill the driver would have to rev up the engine; but when going down it really needed good skills to keep control, and any mistake would result in an accident.

We reached Shuozhou in the evening. It was freezing. Even wrapped in a thick quilt I couldn't sleep. Later we heard that a severe frost had been caused by a belt of cold air moving southward, and that some crops had died of the frost.

Under the bridge on which we were installing our joints there was a clear river. The water was so clean that I could see the bottom. We often washed our clothes and sometimes had a bath in the river.

The construction work had been done in a series of stages. We were there to install the expansion joints. But later we were asked to seal them as well. We had no choice but to carry on. After 17 days, we completed our work and went home.

A Chinese saying goes that "Read 10,000 books and travel 10,000 miles." Although I have not read many books, I have traveled a lot and learned a lot that is talked about in books. In some ways I'm a winner, but in others I'm a loser. I do still regret that I've not learnt more from books.

I'm now a freelancer. I have mastered several skills and can put them to use at different times. After working for six years for other people, I have changed my way of thinking. When I graduated from middle school, I thought it didn't matter how much money I earned. But later it came time to build a house, put together a dowry, and find a wife. I felt myself under ever greater pressure. If a person can live to the age of 70, six years must be nothing. And although I don't have much at the moment, I can create more wealth with my most important asset – youth.

My Wife

For the Middle-autumn Festival in 2004, I got home in the evening after a long journey from Dongguan. As soon as I got home, Mom arranged for me to meet a marriage partner. If I had not come back that very day, I would have missed a good wife. We met, chatted, and got to know each other. We swapped telephone numbers. And later we often called each other. In 2005, the 29th day of the ninth month of the lunar calendar was my birthday. She was working in Beijing while I was in Hangzhou. That evening, she called me while I was working. The machine was noisy and I had set my phone to vibrating mode, so that I didn't pick up her call. The next day she called me again. This time I heard, and seeing her name, I immediately answered the call. Although we talked for only a short while, it felt very sweet.

Look, this is my wedding photo. I keep it in my mobile phone. I don't think marriage an obstacle to my career. It is destiny. Marriage is no excuse for lack of achievement, and it should not hinder your career progress. When you meet hardships, your wife will give you suggestions; when you are tired, she will cook for you; when you are busy with work, she will wash your clothes for you. Although she may not help you much in your career, she will keep your mind from trivial things.

My Dream

Recently, I have come to understand the importance of a good education. Let me show you something. A few days ago, my wife brought this book from her parents' home. The title is *Story with My Two Sons*. The author, Zhao Shaoqin, is her grandfather's brother. Look at these pictures. This is their family photo, and this is a photo of their two sons as children. These were taken in foreign countries. The author works at a publishing house in Harbin and his two sons are promising young men: one attended the Beijing Institute of Technology, and the other Harbin University of Science and Technology. After graduation, they went to study abroad. The elder son worked hard and three universities offered a full scholarship; he finally chose the State University of New York. The younger one was enrolled into the University of Birmingham with a full scholarship. Reading about their success, I have come to understand what education really means.

When I was at school, I imagined a bright future for myself, but reality has not matched my hopes. Over the years, I have realized that the biggest drawback is shortage of money. Society is pragmatic; if you don't have money, there are many things you cannot do, such as building a house or getting married. My pocket is as empty as my face is clean, so what can I do? Look at what I am now. The major reason is that I did not study hard. A good education opens doors to a brighter future, at least brighter than the one I have now.

Now my greatest dream is to earn more money so as to satisfy my wife's wishes, which are to enable my child to study at better schools, and to provide a more comfortable life for my parents. Everyone should have aspirations. Although your aims may not be easy to achieve, you can turn them into reality through your own hard work.

I Don't Belong to the South

Narrator: Wu Xiaolong, male, 19, from Hongan County of Huanggang City, Hubei Province
Job: auto mechanic – worker in a diamond factory – worker in a shoe factory
Work place: Wuhan, Hubei Province – Shenzhen, Guangdong Province

Drop-out

I made the decision to quit school at the end of the weeklong National Day holiday in 2004. I thought it over for a long time while I was at school. I made several phone calls to my primary school classmates who were migrant workers in Shenzhen. They said they all regretted having quit middle school. I wondered whether in the years to come I would have the same feeling. I didn't know what kind of life was awaiting me, and whether I would turn numb like them and waste my life away. I began to feel nervous. But I knew very well that my elder brother, who was studying in a college, had to ask my family for the tuition fees, that my mother had just been discharged from hospital, and that my father was getting older by the day. My teacher had urged me to pay my tuition fees several times.

When I was a child, in a homework essay I once described my parents as a wall which could shelter us from wind and rain. But now, this wall was on the verge of collapse. I told my decision to my parents after supper. My father was shocked – the news provoked a fit of the tobacco-inspired coughing that had never troubled him in decades. I showed him my exam results and pretended to smile, saying, "Look, it's not working out. I have tried my best to study, and I find it difficult to concentrate in class, especially in English. So I don't see any hope that I can pass the university entrance exam." I made believe that I wasn't all that bothered about it, and simply stared at the TV. My father said nothing, and continued to smoke.

I told him that I had done my best, but had nevertheless fallen from 18th place to 48th place in the class. I had no chance of passing the university entrance exam, so I planned to be a migrant worker.... My friends Baoliang and Shitou, neither of whom had finished junior high school, were making a better living as migrants. In contrast to them, I had finished two years of senior high school. I would follow suit to head south, to somewhere like Shenzhen or Dongguan.

Late into the night, I chatted in my bed with my brother about campus life. He told me that life in college was quite free, and that there were lots of school activities. All sorts of books were available in the library. These books helped ease the daily burden of class work. He finished by trying to encourage me, "If you study hard right now, you'll do fine when you get to university." I told him I would. And it was true that a part of me yearned for university life and its lively activities, and the spacious libraries where I could read my favorite books.

After seeing off my brother, I went to school. I offered my books to my classmates, packed up the rest of my belongings, and went home. I remember that my mother cried and said it was all her fault for being a burden to her son. I said nothing as I sorted out my things.

A Pointless Apprenticeship

After a few days at home, my father asked his friends to help me get an apprenticeship as an auto mechanic. I would be supplied with three meals a day, accommodation and 150 yuan a month. My father urged me to learn this skill and make a living out of it, now that I had quit school. I took him up on his suggestion and left home. My destination was Wuhan, a big and chaotic city. Skyscrapers stood side by side with simple huts roofed with tiles.

My master seemed happy with the 20 *jin* of peanut oil and a huge Coca-cola bottle of sesame oil that my father had asked me to bring to him. He told me that I would succeed as long as I worked hard. I smiled at the thought that my life was about to get better. There was a fellow apprentice, who had arrived several months before me. We shared a room and had meals together, and soon became close friends. He had studied only six months in middle school, as his father thought study a waste of time once you could read a few words and road signs. So he had gone to Shenzhen and became a migrant worker at the age of 14. Now he had come back to learn a skill, and to marry some girl whose whereabouts he didn't even know right now.

My master lived with his parents. Time passed quickly and for the first month I was occupied with trifles like sweeping the floor and washing vegetables. Occasionally I accompanied my master to watch him repairing cars. I felt frustrated, but remembered my father's words at my departure: if I wanted to learn a skill, I would have to start at the bottom. So I put up with the housework for three months. I thought my brother would be short of money at the end of the semester, so I mailed 350 yuan to him. When I called him, he wept and said that it should be me who was studying in the college. I said this was out of the question, and that it was too difficult for me to pass the university entrance exam. I wept too after I hung up the phone. But I held on to my belief that I had to learn a skill well to earn as much money as possible.

I lived with my fellow apprentice in the loft of my master's workshop. The convex loft was low inside, so we often bumped our heads. We didn't go home during the Spring Festival as this was a busy period. I had the feeling that my master was reluctant to teach us his trade. He simply required me to buy vegetables and do the housework, and he even asked me to learn to cook, which I did.

One day, as I was about to go into the kitchen to start the cooking, my master's wife started to question me about money I had been given for buying vegetables. I was surprised, and told her that I had put the change in the drawer of the cupboard. She said, "I gave you a 50 yuan note this morning as I had no small change, and it shouldn't have cost more than 20 yuan for the vegetables." "Actually, it only cost 11 yuan," I answered. "So where are the other 39 yuan?" she asked. I repeated that I had put them in the drawer of the cupboard. She fetched my master and asked him to search me all over, complaining, "I have warned you that we should keep an eye on these village boys – their bodies and hands are so dirty." My master tried to calm her down, "Forget it. It's only 10 yuan."

Not only had I learned nothing for the six months I had been there, and not got home for the Spring Festival, but I had to put up with this. That night, my fellow apprentice told me, "We should get out of here. I saw our master take that 10 yuan to buy cigarettes. He is under the thumb of his skinflint wife. She's the one who wears the trousers, and she treats you like dirt. What is the point of us being here? We do nothing but chores and cooking, as if we were nannies. I've been here for over a year, and so far all I've done is deliver the odd tool to our master." I thought it over, and then we both quit the place where I had hoped to take the first steps on the pathway to my dreams.

The Diamond Factory in the South

My parents wanted me to try another apprenticeship, but I refused and left for the south. I was eager to put myself to the test, and a few days later I found myself in Shenzhen.

At first I had ambitions to find a well-paid job. But a series of failures made clear to me the cruel reality of the outside world. I was confused; I had been led to believe that the streets of the south were paved with gold. But the reality was that it was hard to find a job, especially for someone like me with a limited education. A migrant worker without any skills has to make a living through the sweat of his brow. I had very little money on me, but with the help of one of my fellow villagers I managed to find a job in a diamond factory. The factory guaranteed me a probation period of three months with a monthly salary of 700 yuan, and I accepted without hesitation. Knowing that I would be able to finance my brother's monthly living costs, my heart swelled with pride.

My job was simple; what I had to do was grind tiny diamonds under a magnifier. I sometimes had to stare at the magnifier for the whole day, and back in my dormitory at night I could barely open my eyes through the pain. But I clenched my teeth and put up with it, thinking of my brother's monthly living costs, which came to more than 300 yuan.

I lived with 11 other people in a shabby dormitory. Crowded in this little room in Shenzhen's scorching summer, we were plagued by mosquitoes which were impervious to our mosquito nets. We were often woken by their stings by midnight. But we simply put up with it, getting back to sleep by covering our heads with sheets – we had to be up for work the next day. When the heat woke us up, I would think back to the days of my childhood at home: we didn't have an electric fan, so when my siblings and I lay in bed at night, our mother would keep the mosquitoes away by waving a big cattail leaf fan. We would quickly fall asleep with a cool breeze wafting over us from head to toe.

But here the reality was that I was often awoken again no sooner than I had fallen asleep. I struggled to get up in the mornings, and gave myself no more than a quick wash. Then off to work, one eye closed while I stared at the magnifier with the other. After three months many people suffered from dry and aching eyes, with the result that they failed their probation period and were fired. But I survived, and my salary was raised to 850 yuan a month in my fourth month. I felt very pleased with myself; my parents would have to sell a great deal of grain to earn 850 yuan in a year. I thought that maybe I should stay in the south.

I still harbored ambitions, although I had decided to stay in the factory. But soon afterward the factory created a rule that all workers had to deposit one month's salary as a guarantee against leaving without notice. In the two months that followed, the factory began to withhold our salaries, claiming a shortage of working capital. As a result, many workers left, without the agreement of the factory, so they lost their guarantee deposits.

I also resigned, due to increasing problems with my eyes. I didn't secure agreement either, and ended in the same situation as the others, but I had no choice but to leave as my eye problems were getting serious. Now, looking back, I see that I was naïve to resign when I didn't have another job to go to.

After mailing some money to my family I was left with only 200 yuan. As I walked the streets with my sparse bags, I felt lonely in my failure to make myself part of this rich southern city. It was prosperous but cold, and I didn't belong here. Standing on the busy street, and looking at bright lamps glittering in warm windows, I could imagine other people enjoying family comforts in front of the TV together. What could I do now? I didn't even have a place to rest my head.

Finding a New Job

I had never really taken a good look at this strange city before. Standing by the roadside with my baggage, I felt like crying. This was the life I had lived since I left school. At dawn, seeing a bag-lady collecting throwaway plastic cups, I began to think about how many cups she had to collect to earn a single yuan. From then on I became very thrifty; whenever I spent money I would think of her.

Finally, when I was almost down to my last cent, I found a new job. My new job was cutting soles in a shoe factory. Again there was a probation period of three months. My basic wage was 600 yuan per month, with a piece-rate bonus. The more I toiled, the more I earned. In addition, overtime was paid separately.

I soon got the hang of my new job, and worked hard to increase my earnings. There was little to do during our free time, so my colleagues would go shopping to buy clothes at weekend. Sometimes I went out with them. Although my exertions could bring me as much as 1,200 yuan a month, I was unsatisfied. I was repeating the same task every day like a machine – going to work, eating my meals and going to sleep. Sometimes I would panic when thinking about my life. Every time I looked at my books neatly stacked on a corner shelf, I would call my brother. He still felt sorry for me, and once told me, "You mustn't throw your books away, or you will really turn out to be a failure. You should better yourself in spare time – do things like reading, playing ball games and learning other skills. Do you want to be a migrant worker for the rest of your life? What about in 10 or 20 years' time? How will you take care of yourself when you are old? You need to improve your skills while you're young."

My brother first spoke to me in Mandarin, then he switched to our local dialect.

After that call, I suddenly realized that my ambition had gradually drained away. Flicking through my books, I could barely understand them. One reason was that I was tired out by my work, and the other was that I had forgotten most of what I had learned, especially my beloved English. Sometimes I would grow anxious. But looking to the long term, I decided that once my brother had graduated, I would apply myself to learning a skill to feed my family. For the time being I would endure my dull and robotic task. But in my spare time I would read magazines and play ball games to keep my mind awake.

My 18th Birthday

Many of my colleagues in our factory were addicted to playing online games in the Internet cafes. It cost them an enormous amount of money, and I seldom went to such places. The truth was that I missed the routine of my school life with all my heart. And I knew that many of my old classmates would have the chance to become envied students at top universities. But I still had no clear ideas about my own future, and carried on like a robot with my boring work in this southern town where I had lost myself.

After I had finished my overtime one night, I opened my case and took out my old reading books. I realized that there were many articles which I never read before. When I found one of my test transcripts folded in the book, tears ran down my cheek. I folded it up again, put it in the bottom of my case, and went to shower.

After my shower, one of my roommates told me that my brother had just called me, and he would call back later. So I stayed by the phone. I wanted to chat with my brother, but I was afraid of his mentioning examinations and technical schools.

My brother said, "Xiaolong, today is your 18th birthday and you're a grown up. Do you have any plans for your life?" I was astonished. I hadn't even realized today was my birthday. How could I suddenly have turned 18 years old? I could hardly believe it. I answered, "Yes, I do have a plan. After you graduate next year I will learn to become a chef. It seems that people like to spend money on good food." My brother said, "Well, just do whatever you please, as long as it's something that you really want to do." We also talked about our family. He told me my parents had dug a well in our courtyard which was nine m deep. He told me that he was now getting a scholarship of several hundred yuan from his college, and asked me to mail my money to our parents instead for them to hire an engineer to complete the rest of the project. My father was in his fifties, and if the well was completed, he wouldn't have to climb up and down the hillside to fetch water any more.

After hanging up, I decided to go eating out to celebrate my birthday. But the gates of the factory were already closed. So I spent the evening of my 18th birthday crouched under my quilt and missing my family. I recalled my father growing vegetables; my elder brother and I helped him water them. While my mother was cooking I would chat with her while stoking the oven with firewood. I also missed the pleasure of our whole family sitting down together to enjoy a meal.

I had a day off at the weekend, and visited one of my fellow villagers. He and his wife had left their child at home and came out to work. There were many people in a similar situation. Most people planned to work as migrants for seven or eight years, then return to their homes to build their own houses, help their sons find wives, and spend their old age in peace. Sometimes, I was scared by these thoughts – would their children travel the same exhausting path as their parents: marry a wife, work as migrants for seven or eight years, and go back to help their sons find wives? Would this kind of cycle carry on from generation to generation forever?

In the past, I particularly hated being called a countryman. Today, I don't mind it at all. Sometimes I think rural areas are different from urban areas, and there is a huge gap between them, although we are always told that all human beings are created equal. Actually, the gap caused by the accident of birth is still far-reaching.

Thinking of this in the bus, I told myself that I must keep my children from repeating this miserable and unstable life. The same sun shone down on bus passengers like me, on people who carried briefcases, and on pedestrians. I envied people who owned a car. Looking at those skyscrapers, I wished that some day I could dress as neatly as they did and ride my car to work every day at a fixed time. If my wish came true, I would be very contented. However, reality had always confounded my hopes. I had known it was only a dream even back when I was a student. The reality was I was bound to an oily machine in a workshop and my every tomorrow would be the same as the day before.

I was very happy to see my fellow villager, Xiang. We went to buy vegetables together. Although he was nearly 10 years older than me, there was no generation gap between us. We bought lots of vegetables, and from cleaning our vegetables to eating our meal we talked about our work, our lives, and the changes in our families over time. I asked him why he had chosen this way of life. He answered that it was for survival, and for the sake of their child. I disagreed, "But the government now covers primary and junior middle school tuitions, and growing crops also gets government subsidies." He said, "The situation is not quite as clear as that, and it is more complicated than you think. After all, we're from rural areas."

Suddenly, I remembered that when I was a child, I often looked with my elder brother for the location of our village on the torn map in our school's library. We had never succeeded in finding it. My brother said it was because we were surrounded by mountains and forests, and because we lived in a rural area. I didn't understand the difference between rural areas and urban areas. Did people in rural areas have to stay in their homes for the whole of their lives?

Xiang's wife said she would introduce a girlfriend to me. I refused her kind offer. I said I was only 19 years old, and I wanted to wait till I was 20 before looking for a girlfriend.

Farewell to the South

When I called my mother, she told me that a lad from our village who had quit school at the age of 15 or 16 also wanted to find a job in the south. He wanted me to use my social connections and help him find a job. The request filled me with a feeling of helpless anger. I earned money for my family every month through hard labor; I had no "social connections." My toil had nothing to do with brain work, but savage strength.

One day, when I was checking shoes by a stitching machine, it suddenly shook crazily like a mad bull. I immediately pulled my hands back. But I wasn't quick enough, and I felt an acute pain. My right little finger was bleeding heavily, and I pinched it tightly with my left hand. But to no avail – the blood continued to pour through my fingers. I don't know why, but I always feel intense pain at the sight of blood. I wondered miserably whether I was about to die in the south. My tears flowed. My colleagues hurriedly ran over to me and the manager on duty also came over. He drove my colleagues off and ordered them to get back to work. Then he looked at my injured finger and said, "It's nothing, just a bruise."

He brought me to the factory infirmary, and while we were there he made a cell phone call to someone. I didn't hear what was said. After my wound was bandaged, he said I just needed few days rest as the injury was not serious. But I was still in severe pain, and I asked him to take me to hospital for an examination. He said that it was nothing but a bruise, and that this sort of thing often happened in the factory.

According to the labor contract, injured workers should be provided with an examination of the wound, or given a disability determination by the factory. Over the next few days, the factory ignored my request for a disability determination. The pain in my finger grew steadily worse, and I knew it was not a bruise, so I decided to go to hospital for a disability determination by myself.

The disability determination process was complicated. Without any support from the factory, I had to take my application to the social security office that provided insurance cover to my factory. Then I had to go to the district social security office to carry out relevant procedures, followed by a visit to the appointed hospital for the determination. This meant that the examination I had previously had was disqualified, and I had to pay my own fees for the new examination. The manager warned me that I was to cover all costs up to half a month's salary, if the result was not in my favor. I thought if I was going to go ahead, I should do it without any hesitation.

I didn't tell my family that I was injured. Instead I called my brother and told him that I was planning to sit the Self-study Examination for Higher Education. He said he would give his full support and help me get hold of study materials. The result of disability determination would come out in a month. So while waiting for the result I used the time to study English and mathematics. I thought I would soon be able to go home, and I could learn how to cook while preparing for the exam. I couldn't help becoming excited as I allowed my imagination to run free.

Finally I got the result. I had been accorded 10th-class disability status. I was a lucky one among the unlucky. When I went to the factory for my last social security benefits, my colleagues told me that many workers' fingers had been injured, and some even cut off, while operating those aging machines. The boss would usually solve this by compensating the injured. I hated this way of hushing the whole thing up through a surreptitious payment. It would prevent any proper investigation from taking place.

My brother tells me that there are two kinds of people among both students and migrant workers: the first kind have no ambition; the second never stop working hard to achieve their dreams. I know that I will come back some day as my transcript is accompanying me all the time. I don't belong to the south, because it belongs to someone else.

To Be an Independent Woman

Narrator: Xiao Xiaohong, female, 27, from Qijiang Town of Longhui County, Hunan Province
Job: warehouse keeper – secretary – clerk
Work place: Guangzhou – Shenzhen, Guangdong Province

I was born into a poor family; my parents are thrifty farmers. Rice-growing is the only source of income in my home village. Like many secluded rural areas, people there are conservative in their views. A failure to appreciate education, and valuing men while devaluing women, are deeply-rooted traits. I have two elder sisters, one elder brother and one younger sister. My parents are more enlightened than their fellow villagers, and they wished my siblings and I could go to school, though it would cost them much toil. In order to finance our school fees, they busied themselves day and night on the farm. However, it was impossible to pay the costs for the whole family, as tuition fees depended on the output of several rice patches. Our life was hard.

My eldest sister studied hard, and she went on to nursing school after graduating from junior high school. My second sister was very naughty and did not like reading. She was in the third-grade in primary school when my eldest sister passed the exam for nursing school. My family couldn't afford tuition fees for both of them, and so my second elder sister had to drop out of school and help my parents with the farm work. My father wished his son could go on to university. But my brother fell in love while still young, and he failed the college entrance examination. So he left for the south and became a migrant worker. By that time my eldest sister had graduated from nursing school and become a nurse. She had a monthly salary of 600 yuan – not a huge sum, but it was a secure job. My brother, then 19, had acquired no particular skills, so he had to sell his labor on a construction site. He toiled there and lived in poor conditions.

That left just me and my younger sister, who were both able to attend school. Both of us studied very hard in hope of getting to university and being able to escape from the village. But when I was in junior middle school, it became clear that it would be impossible for the family to find the money for both of us to go to university. Besides, my parents suffered poor health, and they were getting worse with each day that passed. So I decided to go to a secondary technical school to study accounting after graduating from junior middle school. The sooner I found a job, the smaller the burden my parents would have to bear. I thought it ought to be easy to find a job as long as I had a worthwhile qualification.

My cousin, who had been a migrant worker in Guangzhou for two years, came back home just around my graduation from the secondary technical school. I asked her lots of questions about Guangzhou, and whether her job was strenuous…. She didn't go into any detail in her answers, "You're well educated and you will easily find a well-paid job, compared with the situation in our hometown." Indeed, anyone who graduated from junior high school would be considered well educated. Most people went no further than primary school, and some didn't even finish that. In our home village girls like me were usually sent out to look for work before they even finished primary school. Nothing could be done to change this contemptible tendency to value men while devaluing women.

First Impression of Guangzhou

On August 15, 2000, I came to Guangzhou along with my cousin. That first night, I slept in a house rented by her and her two colleagues. Each of them paid 50 yuan per month for this 40-sq-m earthen house. The bed, made of a few wooden boards, provided me with a hard night.

When I got up the next morning, I was aching all over. The mosquitoes had left their "souvenirs" all over my face. I decided to take a rest first, and try my luck in the nearby factories in the afternoon. I took a pen and paper with me to write down the names of the streets, as I was well aware that I was no longer in my home village, and would probably lose my way if I was careless. I visited a few factories, but found none that was looking to recruit. This was disappointing, as I needed to find a job as quickly as possible. I had very little money, and would find myself starving if I spent it. Although I was in the company of my cousin, I didn't want to rely on her because she was not rich herself, and her own family was poor too. All her hard-earned money was mailed to her younger brother, who was a student.

However, it was not easy to find a job. In order to save money I hadn't eaten any breakfast, and I was exhausted by the time I got back to the house.

On the second day, I went out again. I prayed that I could find something. I walked a good distance – over three km from my cousin's home. There were several small mills in the area and I tried them one by one. I soon found that my qualifications didn't match their needs. So, I decided to take whatever job I could find to get myself started.

I eventually came to a big factory, and asked a security guard what they produced. He told me they produced works of art in wood, and he also told me that interns would be paid 500 yuan a month, with accommodation provided.

Knowing now what the situation was, I decided to take my chance in this company. I came back and excitedly told my cousin my plan. But she was not in favor, "You won't stay long in that factory – the job won't suit you. I know this factory, because one of my friends once worked there." But I insisted, "I don't want to waste any more time. I'd rather give this place a try. As long as accommodation is provided, I think I can make a go of it." She eventually gave her agreement, rather than waiting in the hope that a more suitable job would turn up.

Taking the Job

I went to the factory with my ID card and my graduation certificate next day.

The recruiting officer was a man in his forties. He asked me amiably, "It can't be long since you graduated – how old are you?"

"Would you like to have a guess?" I replied.

He smiled, "You're 19 years old." I also smiled, without saying yes or no.

In fact, I didn't have to go through any examination, or the complicated interviewing procedures that I had expected. He let me sign a contract and said to me after checking my ID card, "So you're from Hunan? There are lots of others from Hunan here. Work hard, and I will promote you if a well-paid job in the office comes up."

I had never expected that finding my first job would go so smoothly. At first, I didn't understand why this man was treating me so well. As a fresh girl just out of school, I was delighted to have found a job so quickly. I felt surprised as well as lucky. I learned that this man was the boss of the company, and his name was Xiao. On August 17, 2000, I started my working career. A superintendent took me to my workplace on the second floor. As my major in school was accounting, I was assigned to the warehouse. He gave me my job: to keep count of products.

When I came in, all the girls in the place stared at me, and I heard all sort of whispers: "Look at this beautiful girl, why would she want to work here – she graduated from a secondary technical school....? I bet she will leave soon.... She won't be able to cope with the workload...." I kept my head down and dared not even make eye contact with the others. I simply told myself that I would do a good job. These people talking about me in this way knew nothing of my situation. I could do the job as well as they did. I told myself that I shouldn't let them look down on me.

I had a fellow worker, named Xiaohong, in the warehouse. She treated me very kindly. She taught me how to count and earnestly explained the procedures to me, though it was really very simple. However, I was on my feet all day long, shuttling between the ground floor and the second floor. I quickly grew tired as the time went by.

My daily routine was hard, but dull. There were only three places for me to go: the dormitory, the canteen, and my workplace. I became accustomed to a life spent between these three spots. As the factory had to fulfill whatever orders coming in, we had to work on Sundays too. That meant we didn't have any free time.

An Accident

I will never forget the day – there was a heavy downpour. I had to go to work in afternoon. Exhausted, I didn't get out of my bed until I heard the factory bell. I hurriedly rushed to clock in, otherwise I would be fined and my day's work would be in vain.

But as I hurried to climb the stairs I slipped and fell. I can no longer remember exactly what happened. As I was falling down I felt a sharp pain in my foot, and I lost consciousness.

When I came to, I saw that my boss Xiao was with me. I was told that it was him who had sent me to hospital in his car. He said, "You've finally woken up. I was really worried. Why were you so careless? You're lucky your head isn't badly injured – all you have is a slight concussion. You just need a good rest." Hearing his words, a feeling which I couldn't identify came into my mind – was it a kind of appreciation, or uneasiness, or joy, or shame?

He continued, "It must be painful as your ankle is sprained. Don't worry – I'll stay with you." I was almost moved to tears by his words, but I held myself in check. I didn't know why my boss, a man in his forties, was taking care of me like this. I knew it was unusual. I didn't know what to think – I was very naïve. I thought it was very kind of him.

Xiaohong came by that evening to make sure that I was all right. I felt very grateful to her and said, "I'm sorry to be such a nuisance – I'll buy you a good dinner when I'm better." But Xiaohong grinned at me conspiratorially, "No, you needn't do that. But please don't forget me after you're transferred to the office!" "You'll always be my friend, no matter where I work," I said. "How could I forget you? But I don't know anything about being transferred to the office. " She kept her mysterious smile and said, "It will be soon.... People in our factory are talking about you today. They're saying Mr Xiao has fallen in love with you. It's the first time he's ever sent a girl to hospital in his car. You're beautiful as well as well-educated – you're different from the other girls. They think you'll soon be transferred to the office."

I was confused and said, "Is there anything wrong? Isn't it normal that the boss should take care of his workers?"

But Xiaohong retorted, "It's not in the least normal. I've been here for three years, and I've never seen him so concerned with a girl. You're lucky. "

I was completely taken aback by Xiaohong's words. I was no longer sure whether my boss' kindness to me came from his appreciation of my ability. He had indeed said that he would promote me if the opportunity arose. Was there some less than straightforward reason for his kindness to me? As a fresh 19-year-old girl who had just graduated from school I hardly knew what to say. I just thought I should believe in myself. It was definitely a good thing that my boss appreciated my ability, and I certainly wanted a promotion and a job in the office. But I couldn't help wondering why this opportunity had arrived so suddenly, and it made me nervous.

I was confused and said to Xiaohong, "Forget about it. Let's talk about you. I really don't know anything about you. Are you married?" She told me that she had married young, and she had a seven-year-old child. Her husband was a construction worker. She had left to become a migrant worker when her baby was one year old. Her mother-in-law was looking after the child. She was loath to leave her child alone in the village, but the need to find money for its upbringing left her with no other choice. "Don't marry young," she exhorted me. "Earn as much money as possible while you're young. Open a small store in the future – that's better a life as a migrant worker."

I really appreciated Xiaohong's advice. But life can be hard. I had been through hardship myself after I graduated from school. And I could have been killed in this accident. There is no guarantee that life will be secure for ever.

Promoted to Secretary

After four days in hospital, I asked to be discharged, as my head was better and my foot was no longer troubling me much.

That day, Mr Xiao came to pick up me and invited me to dinner. I said, "Thank you for your invitation, but I am afraid that people in the company will talk about it behind my back." "It's nothing," he reassured me. "You needn't bother about them. I will be disappointed if you refuse me."

I couldn't find the right words to say no, so I went to a restaurant with him. We sat and had tea before the meal. He asked me why I hadn't gone to college. I replied that my family situation didn't allow it. He said, "There are many young people in situations like yours. You have done a good job. There are only two university-graduates in our office, and a few people who graduated from junior colleges and high schools." He went on to ask me, "Would you like to go to college?" "Of course, but that dream will have to wait until I have improved my situation and earned some money. Right now, my family situation won't allow it. I have a younger sister and I want her to go to college."

"Would you go to college if I paid your fees?"

I was struck dumb. All sorts of thoughts ran through my mind: Although I was very grateful to him, I couldn't understand why he would help me like this, and why he treated me so well. I understood quite clearly that there is no such thing as a free lunch, and I wondered what his purpose was; I told myself that I shouldn't accept such a reward, offered without any effort on my part. So I refused him politely, "Thank you for your kindness. I can't go to college now, because my family relies on me to support them."

He smiled gently, "No problem. I understand your situation. I'm planning to appoint you as my secretary next month. What do you say?"

I really wanted this post, but I replied, "I'm not qualified for such a post. I'd like to have a try as an accountant or cashier."

He shook his head, "I believe you're capable of doing the job well; what you need to do is deal with one or two matters, and prepare meeting reports. It's not difficult and I can teach you how to do it. You just need a little preparation."

We started our meal. He ordered chicken soup with ginseng, especially to help my recovery. All the dishes he ordered were special. I felt uneasy as he offered me food. I never had a meal with a man alone – and furthermore, this was my boss.

After a week's rest, I went back to my work. That day, the head of the personnel department smiled knowingly at me and said, "Congratulations, Miss Xiao! You're our new secretary now." At that very moment, Mr Xiao also came over, "Let me explain your new duties."

"Will I really be up to the job?" I asked nervously.

"Of course you will," he nodded. "Please put your heart into your work. Your monthly salary will be 2,100 yuan."

I couldn't believe my ears. I felt very excited, and very nervous. It was incredible that my salary had been increased to over 2,000 yuan from only 600 yuan. But it was true. As well as my momentary excitement, I felt a pang of unease.

Departure

As a new graduate fresh from school, I had never expected to earn 2,000 yuan a month. So I was determined to work all the harder to merit this hard-earned job. But as secretary I anticipated a lot of pressure. After all, I had just graduated from secondary technical school, and there would be a lot to learn.

My boss seemed to understand the pressure I felt, and told me to take things step by step, and ask him for help if I had any problem. I was encouraged by his words; I never thought that a boss would treat his subordinate so kindly. I tried to put aside any growing suspicions.

Things proceeded smoothly, and I got along well with my colleagues. Soon it was New Year. Over the last days of 2001, we received our year-end bonuses.

One morning, I was alone with him in the office. He handed a bulging red envelope to me, smiling mysteriously and saying, "This is your bonus and you've earned it with your excellent work." I took the envelope and opened it. There was a lot of money – at least 5,000 yuan, all in a bundle. I couldn't understand why he had given me so much, "I should only get an extra month's salary. Why have you given me so much?" He said, "You should see it as an encouragement. I will increase your salary as long as you work hard."

I knew it clearly that my boss was giving me special favors. I also knew it clearly that many secretaries had been lovers of their bosses. Over time, I grew to understand what Mr Xiao really wanted. But I would never become a man's lover for the sake of his wealth and social status. I appreciated Mr Xiao very much for the fact that he valued me and helped me. But my feelings for him were limited to the respect and appreciation from a subordinate to her supervisor, and had nothing to do with the affection between men and women. And Mr Xiao always treated me with respect, and never made any improper advances to me.

On May 12, 2001, Mr Xiao asked me to accompany him to a wedding dinner for the son of one of his friends. For the special occasion he bought me an evening dress – something I had never worn in my life. But I couldn't refuse his kindness.

The dinner was luxurious and he had a lot to drink. I tried to persuade him not to drink so much, as he had to drive home. He said he wanted to drink his fill because he was so happy. I couldn't prevent him. By the end of the dinner, he was clearly drunk. His friend wouldn't allow him to drive, and arranged for a room for him in the hotel. I was mortified at the thought that I would have to stay and look after him. I couldn't leave him alone in the hotel, but how embarrassing to have to stay with him. And I was worried that something improper would occur. His friend told me, "Miss Xiao, I'm entrusting your boss to you – please take good care of him."

I was in a terrible dilemma. But I had no choice, so I helped my boss to his room. To my shock, he grabbed my hands as soon as we entered the room, mumbling, "Do you know I fell in love with you the first time I saw you? I've never said anything to you because I respect you. I know you should never force your love on somebody. I know you wouldn't want that...."

In his drunkenness, he said a lot of things. I hadn't actually realized quite how drunk he was. But I am absolutely not the kind of woman who would allow herself to be cajoled into becoming a man's lover. I've never had anything but contempt for women who wreck other people's family life and break up their marriages. None of that was going to change just because this was my boss. And he just wasn't my type.

But he carried on, "If only you would be my girlfriend, I will rent a luxurious house for you. You won't have to work any more, and I'll take care of you. You can have whatever you want...."

Lying on the bed, he continued to talk. I was in tears, and helpless. I really didn't know what to do. But at last, probably because of the drink, he fell asleep. I didn't close my eyes the whole night long. I pondered over many things. I should have known that it was going to happen sooner or later – well, now it had happened. For some girls, it would be a chance to change their life. My boss was rich, and could offer them almost anything they wanted: beautiful clothes, a luxurious home, entertainment. But this was not the kind of love I wanted.

I thought a lot, and by dawn I had made the decision to resign. Although I needed this job, I couldn't stand the thought of making myself the subject of other people's ridicule. I needed money very much, but I wasn't going to cheat myself and sell my dignity and soul. Mr Xiao is not the type of man I wanted. A relationship with a man who was attracted to me by my looks would not last long. That was not going to be my story. I would rather do tiring work and earn an honest living.

The following morning on our way to work, my boss said to me, "Thank you for taking care of me last night, and please forgive me if I did you any wrong. I will not drink alcohol like that again. I was so happy last night; that's why I let myself get drunk."

Back in the office, I handed him my letter of resignation, saying that I was to go back to school that September, as my family situation had improved. "Didn't I ask you whether you wanted to go to college before?" he said, "But you said no. Now I still support you. Will you accept my help to pay for you to go to college?"

I understood only too clearly that if I took his help I would be putting myself under an obligation to him. I didn't want to rely on charity from anyone, so I refused, "I appreciate very much your kindness and all the help you've given me. I am very lucky to have met a boss like you. I'll come back and work for you after I finish my college." He remained silent, a look of disappointment on his face. Then he said, "Well, I am reluctant to let you go, but I can't deprive you of your freedom of choice. Anyhow, please call me or write to me in future and let me know that everything is fine."

I nodded. The truth was that I didn't want to quit the job, and my story about going to college was only an excuse. I knew too that I would never get back in touch with this man. I didn't know why – I just knew I wouldn't do it. But where could I go once I left this company?

Unpredictable Life

I went to Shenzhen, another prosperous city. After three days I found a post as an accountant, with a monthly salary of 1,800 yuan. I worked eight hours a day and six days a week. I was content and

I felt good. Although Mr Xiao had paid me a higher salary, I had always felt uneasy. Now at last I was free of strain and discomfort. I also found a part-time job selling cosmetics. It was hard work. But my tiredness disappeared when I saw my savings growing in my bank account.

In my leisure time, I bought some books about the stock market. I had been told that stocks were the quickest way to earn money. So I planned to learn the ropes, and once I had enough savings I would go into the stock market in pursuit of my first pot of gold. In 2006, I finally invested 30,000 yuan in the stock market. In a rising market, I made some sound choices, and earned a bit of money. But the stock market has its ups and downs, and I worry that I might suffer losses as well.

I wasn't expecting to face any worse misfortune in my life than the volatility of the stock market. But in the summer of 2005, I was stricken by dreadful news: my younger sister was suffering from leukemia. I couldn't believe it. How could God treat us in this way?

My family and I had been so happy and proud when my younger sister passed the college entrance exam in 2003. It was wonderful that our family had finally produced a college student, because that kind of thing never happened in our village.

Now, things were happening so quickly. Only two years after she entered college; now a terrible leukemia was threatening her fragile life. My poor sister had to quit school and receive treatment at home. But as a simple rural family, it was impossible for us to meet the costs of such an expensive treatment. Where could we turn for help to save this dying angel? Finally came the cruel reality – my younger sister was gone. I still can't accept the truth; I still feel that she is alive, just beside me. But where has she gone, and why does she never talk to me any more?

My sister's death was a terrible blow to me. Not only my family, but the whole village was proud of her. But our sadness couldn't save her life. I'll find my way out of the pain, because I know she would not want to see me so miserable. She would often tell me, "Dear, you are the toughest of the lot; don't cry, because you have to provide for the family." I constantly bear her words in mind: live with confidence for her sake and for the sake of my family.

That same year, my second sister got divorced. She had to go out to work to feed her child and had little time to spare to help handle our family affairs. My eldest sister was trying to keep her own marriage going. As a mother of three children, divorce won't be an easy course of action for her.

From the stories of my two elder sisters, I have learned that marriage is volatile. I'm even afraid of getting married. My parents worry about the subject. But I don't want to get into an unhappy marriage like my two sisters. I won't get married just for the sake of it. Anyway, it is difficult for me to find my Mr Right.

For the time being, I just want to earn whatever money I can, to take care of my parents and provide them with a happy old age.

Generally, the hardships I have suffered over the years have helped me understand life's challenges, and how fragile we are. For the moment, the thought of trying to earn a "diploma" is too heavy a burden for me to shoulder. Today, college students can be found everywhere. I feel humble, and I regret that I didn't go to college when I was younger. If I had made better choices, I wouldn't have had to endure so much hardship over those years. Today, I have to work harder than others. But I can cope with that, and I believe that as long as I try my best I will be able to create a happy life for myself.

My greatest wishes are that my parents enjoy good health and live safely, and that I can earn money from my investments. If I have time, I would study to improve myself; for too many years I've been busy with my work and neglected my studies. If I don't acquire new knowledge, sooner or later society will cast me aside. I need to make haste!

From Decoration Worker to Boss

Narrator: Xu Dehua, male, 35, from Hefan Village of Xishui County, Huanggang City, Hubei Province
Job: decoration worker – boss of a decoration company
Work place: Xi'an, Shaanxi Province

I was born in a small mountain village in southeastern Hubei. My forefathers were farmers for generations. Before I was one month old, my father invited his eldest brother to give me a name. My uncle had completed senior high school and was the most educated person in my family. At the feast celebrating my first month, my uncle announced the name he had chosen for me: Dehua. My parents asked what it meant, and he explained, "De means virtue, bearing the hope that he will be a virtuous person; while hua means prosperity, bearing the hope that he will lead a prosperous life with success in his career." My parents were satisfied.

On my first birthday, my parents prepared a ceremony for me. According to tradition, a one-year-old baby should choose from a number of articles offered to him, and the choice he makes will indicate his future profession. If the baby picks up a pen, he might become an intellectual. In the 1970s, the pen was the symbol of the intellectual; anyone with a pen in his pocket looked vigorous. If the baby picks up an abacus, he might become an accountant. At that time, an accountant on a village committee was sometimes even more influential than the village director because he held control of the finances. If the baby chooses rice, he might work on a farm for life. If the baby goes for the cookies, he might turn out to be lazy and dislike work. If the baby chooses a weight, he might become a trader.

As I was to make my choice, my family members wondered anxiously what it would be and what my future might hold. When I grew up, my parents told me that my first choice was a pen. Those present offered their congratulations, saying that our family would have a top scholar. My parents smiled wryly, "Where do we find money for his schooling? Let alone a scholar." But as I went on to choose the weight, the abacus, and the rice, my parents smiled in relief, as they thought farming would offer me a better future.

Hard-won Five-year Education at Primary School

I have brothers and sisters, and I am the youngest child, and therefore the family favorite. When I was eight years old, my eldest sister got married, and one of her betrothal gifts from the bridegroom was to be my first tuition fees. My eldest uncle sent me a new green schoolbag from the city, saying that all children there carried such schoolbags. Mom made a suit of new clothes for me. In the evening before I went to school, I fell asleep carrying my new schoolbag. I had rarely felt such happiness. I wanted to tell everyone around me: I am going to school! I cherished this hard-won opportunity and studied very hard. I also became more helpful around the home; after finishing homework I would assist with housework. During the holidays, I grazed cattle for the village. I usually chose a hill with lush grass, tied the cattle to a tree, and then sat down and studied.

Goodbye to School

I loved school, but cruel reality intervened. As I was to enter Grade Five, the tuition fees rose and my family could no longer afford them. My eldest uncle had given me a lot of financial support over the previous five years, and we could not ask for more. Other relatives were also experiencing financial difficulties. So with a heavy heart I had to put aside my schoolbag, take up the hoe, and go farming with my parents. I was reluctant to leave school, and I carried on reading my old textbooks again and again. But my family was poor and could not pay my tuition fees, so I could not continue schooling. I must earn my own living. But how could I earn money, as a 12-year-old child?

On one occasion I happened to hear that a tiler in our neighboring village was looking for apprentices. Was this not a good opportunity? I wouldn't need to leave home, and could earn 10 cents a day with a meal provided by the employer. Taking two bottles of wine with him, my father accompanied me to the tiler's home. I went through a procedure to honor my master, and became an apprentice tiler. I went to work with my master every morning. My work was to climb onto roofs and lay tiles. It sounded simple, but it demanded skills – I had to make sure that the tiles looked neat and the results were weatherproof. Moreover, the work was dangerous. On one occasion I was working on a moss-covered roof after several days of rain. The roof was slippery and I fell off while working on a corner of an eave. Fortunately, I fell on a pile of straw and was not hurt. I followed this life for two years, and my parents were always in a state of anxiety. I still harbored a wish to go back to school, so after saving some money, I said good-bye to my master.

I started schooling again. To catch up with my peers, I went into Grade Two of a junior high school. I borrowed old textbooks from classmates and studied them by myself. I asked classmates and teachers about anything I did not understand. On advancing to Grade Three, my hope was to get into a good senior high school. With this goal, I studied even harder. Unfortunately, while I was struggling for my dream, my mother fell ill due to overwork. As Mom's favorite child, I could not be selfish. I used the money that I had saved for my tuition fees to pay for a doctor. Mom recovered quickly after a period of treatment and rest. When she could work again, I left school once more, still carrying my schoolbag. I joined the ranks of numerous ordinary farmers.

Encouragement from *The Ordinary World*

Although I had left school, I still enjoyed reading. During slack periods, I read our family's few books, and then borrowed books from others. Over a period of three years, I read more than 30 books, although in rural areas few families owned any books at all, let alone good ones. So I was in the habit of reading every book again and again, until I knew them off by heart. I even copied some good articles. Among these books, Lu Yao's *The Ordinary World* was my favorite. The hero's extraordinary fate touched my heart.

I can still remember a paragraph in the book: "What is life? Life is an unceasing struggle. Once you have set yourself a goal, strive to achieve it and never consider any of your efforts wasted; thus you will lead life to the fullest and remain young at heart." At that time, I had lost my enthusiasm for life. But this paragraph encouraged me, helping me regain my passion for life and set my goals anew.

When I was 19, a group of young people in my village wanted to leave home and go out to see the world. I also had a great longing for a bright future, so I spoke to my parents on the subject. I tried several times to persuade them, and they finally agreed. On the eve of my departure, they exhorted me again and again, "Be polite. Eat well. Work hard…." When I left, they asked my fellow travelers to take care of me as I was a youngster.

After a bumpy journey lasting several days and nights, we reached our destination – Xi'an. We had chosen to come here because we had heard that some people from our neighboring village were working here and earning good money. We made some enquiries, and finally tracked them down. As fellow townsmen, they took us in, and we joined them working on a construction site. I was the youngest and weakest. Every day after work, I was exhausted. It felt like every bone in my body was aching, and I often fell asleep as soon as I lay down on my bed. After a few days, my hands and feet were covered with bleeding blisters. A villager came to my assistance, and pierced the blisters with a heated needle. It was painful. I had not suffered such hardships at home. But I endured them, in pursuit of my dream.

Chancing upon a Good Employer

When our work finished on that particular construction site, we could not find proper jobs. The common practice was that one person should go to wait at the labor market and try to find employers. We talked the thing through and it was agreed that I would be the one. So I went to the labor market every morning, and tried to find an employer among the teeming crowds. I waited for days, but nobody approached me or talked to me. By noon on the fifth day I was so hungry that I went off to a small restaurant and bought a bowl of noodles. When I came back, I saw a boss heading off with several workers. I had missed an opportunity to pick up work. I was filled with regret. That opportunity would have been mine if only I had waited a little longer. To make sure that I did not miss any further opportunities, in the following days I bought steamed buns and a bottle of water in advance, and then waited in the market for the whole day. At noon, I had a lunch of hard, cold buns and cold water. On the 10th day, I finally found some work.

The work was to decorate a house for the client. All of us appreciated this hard-won chance and worked very hard. We completed the work a few days ahead of schedule. The client paid us more than the amount we agreed on to thank us, and invited us to come back and see him again. We were moved by his trust. We had heard that urban residents did not respect migrant workers, regarding us as nothing more than cheap labor. Some employers pocketed a portion of the workers' wages or fell behind in paying them. Some labor contractors or foremen cared nothing for their workers' security and paid little attention to safety precautions. As a result workers would occasionally fall from a height and suffer serious injury; those contractors or foremen would give them a little money in compensation, and disappear. What would these workers live on if they could not work? For many such reasons, we had had misgivings about this employer. How would he treat us? Reality went on to prove that there are more good people than bad ones. We were grateful to him, and he said he would take us on again if he needed hands later.

A Professor's Suggestion

Seeing how rapidly Xi'an was developing, I determined to work here and make a career. I did odd jobs for two years. To save traveling expenses, I only went back once for a Spring Festival, and stayed at home for one month. In 1993, a matchmaker introduced me to a girl from a neighboring village, and I married her that year, at the age of 21. In 1994, my son was born, and as head of my family I felt growing pressure: I must earn more money to support my family. Concerned about my parents, wife and son, I set off to find work again. On days when I had work to do, I felt fulfilled. I used any leisure time to read books, look at family photos, or express my homesickness in letters.

In 2001, my son was seven years old, and ready to start primary school. To give him prospects of a better education, I took him and my wife to Xi'an. In their company, I could work in contentment.

On one occasion I happened to meet Prof Li, a former client in the labor market. He asked me how things were going. On finding that I still had to wait my turn for employment at the marketplace, he felt sympathy for me. He said he had left his job and set up his own company; he was his own boss. He suggested I set a construction company. I asked, "But I'm a farmer. So you really think a farmer can set up his own company?" He answered with a smile, "Why not? I think you have a good head for business. You have worked for many years. Don't you want to make more of yourself?" He then went through with me the process of setting up a company. He said that my workmates could be the first employees. A company would be more competitive than individual workers in the market; through it I could build up a reputation in the industry and a wider and more solid network of relationships, and finally make the company bigger and stronger....

Mr Li's words inspired me. With his help, I looked up relevant documents, and learned that the government gave both policy and capital support to migrant workers, encouraging them to start their own businesses. I also noticed that there were plenty of examples that ended in family breakup or even death.

My parents were old, my wife was weak and my son was young; how could I put aside the pressure on me? As an ordinary migrant worker, I was earning little, but my life was stress-free. This was how I had comforted myself during those days, though I did not feel peace in my heart. I asked myself, "What has happened to all my passion and dreams? I'm still young, and have a long way to go. I'm 30 years old. Confucius said a man should be independent at the age of 30. If I don't make progress now, will I spend the rest of my life as a farmer?" I spoke of my feelings to my family and they supported me. The problem was this: how could I, with only seven years of schooling and no capital, set up and run a company? Capital was the most direct issue, and the hardest. In the succeeding days, I thought over this constantly, and found myself trapped in a dilemma.

I turned to Mr Li for help. He offered me advice, "Anyone who starts a new business will meet difficulties and have misgivings. But if you don't try, how can you know if you would have succeeded? And don't worry about capital. I can lend you some and you can borrow from relatives, or even apply for loans from any bank. The problem will be settled. As for management, I can see you're a diligent and studious young man; you need to read plenty of books and learn how others manage and run a company, and then apply those theories in practice and learn more through your work…." Hearing what he said, I thought he was my bosom friend and teacher. I did not know how to thank him, but I could prove in reality that I would not disappoint him, or my family!

A Path Full of Twists and Turns

I read several books on management, and made ready plans to set up my company. In 2002, with others' help and financing from different channels, I registered a construction company. My first business was to decorate a big beauty salon for Mr Li. In the first six months, my company earned 400,000 yuan. It was the first time I had ever seen so much money. I returned the money that I had borrowed from relatives, and sent 50,000 yuan to my parents. Moreover, I had our 40-year-old earth-brick house pulled down and replaced with a two-storey building in my hometown, and I bought some home appliances – my house took on an entirely new look.

In 2003, I bought a cross-country vehicle for 100,000 yuan. It made things convenient for business. For the Spring Festival, I drove home with my wife and child, and did not feel tired on the way. When I got home, fellow villagers came to our house and looked at my car. My parents were delighted at their reaction, "Dehua is so capable! Look, he has built a new house and bought a car."

However, life is not always tranquil. In 2004, I got a piece of work: to decorate a block of apartments. Unfortunately, a lack of safety awareness in construction resulted in an accident: a worker fell from a height when setting up scaffolding and was seriously injured. I immediately sent him to hospital, paid all the fees and wired 50,000 yuan to his family – thus I dealt with this accident properly. The experience taught me a lesson. After the accident, I gave top priority to issues of safety whenever I inspected a construction site and when I held meetings. I studied relevant safety regulations, and then explained them to workers, so that all my employees were conscious of the importance of safety. Thanks to these measures, no other accidents happened during this work.

After eight months of effort, I completed decorating the whole building. But when it was time to get payment, I could not find any trace of the owner. Who would come up with the 1.2 million yuan I was due? My employees needed their money to go home for Spring Festival. I wanted to safeguard our migrant workers' interests by legal means. I brought an action against the owner at the local bureau of labor arbitration. Local law-enforcement departments carried out an investigation and found out that he had run up debts due to an addiction to gambling, and fled. Would this mean that our workers would get nothing for eight months' hard work? I tried my best to avoid that. A local court sold the apartment block at auction to repay the owner's debts. Finally I got part of the money. The first thing I did was to pay workers their wages and pay back supplies invoices that I had defaulted on. Once all these expenses had been deducted, I did not earn much that year. But I did not lose heart. At least I had learned several lessons: pay top priority to safety; sign a reasonable and standard contract before construction; and offer medical insurance for workers to better ensure their and my interests.

I Bought a Home in the City

In the latter half of 2005, to save costs, I opened a shop selling construction materials, bought a truck for transportation, and hired several university graduates to help me run my company. During the first month, the shop's turnover was not good and I lost money. To improve business, I contacted some construction companies and offered them quality products at lower prices. Trusting in my good word, these companies started to use my materials, and finally became my faithful clients. The shop developed in an orderly fashion, and soon made up the deficits and started to turn a profit. I earned a decent amount of money.

In 2006, I said goodbye to rental charges, and bought myself a house in the suburbs of Xi'an. By that time, I had worked for 15 years away from home. From first sleeping out on the street, through living in dark and damp sheds, from renting a cheap small house to buying my own home, I had succeeded in improving my standard of living. In the latter half of that year, the house was decorated. With workmates' help, my family moved in. I finally owned my own home in this big city, and I was so happy that I found it hard to convey my feelings in words.

I hope to build up my company in the future, and find my place in the market of Xi'an. Modern Xi'an has a prosperous economy and a beautiful environment, and the government has publicized preferential policies – all these offer a good platform for our migrant workers.

I want to tell those who are going to work away from home: the first thing you should learn is to bear hardship and withstand hard work – understand that success comes from effort; the second is to keep studying in life, acquire new knowledge, enrich yourself, advance with the times, and turn yourself into a knowledgeable professional; and third, treat your work with care and attention, and build wealth with your own efforts. For myself, my principle is to live a full life and I always use it to encourage myself.

A Life Combining Work and Study

Narrator: Zheng Bo, male, 35, from Wangren Town, Huangshi City, Hubei Province
Job: porter – manager – student of a night university
Work place: Shenzhen, Guangdong Province

Unwilling to Teach at a Primary School

In 2002 at the age of 20, I graduated from a local teachers' school. But overall my school record was not very good and I had dreams of the outside world. I decided to discontinue my studies and go to Shenzhen.

When I told my mother what I was thinking, she disagreed. She had hoped that I could carry on with my schooling, put an end to the misfortunes of farming life, and find a regular job. But she knew that I could not get into university with low academic scores, and so could do nothing about my apathy toward school.

To keep me at home, my family used their connections to get me a job at a nearby primary school. In a matter of weeks, I realized that I could not get used to such a wretched life: I had to be up at dawn and come home at dusk; at work, I was confronted with naughty children and chalk dust; and the wage was so low that some colleagues said it was barely enough to buy cigarettes. I did not live in the school, but traveled between home and school every day. I had no passion for such a dull but demanding life, and so again I formed the idea of going away to work.

To achieve my purpose, I used both hard and soft approaches with my mother, but to no avail. She simply complained about my continuing to bother her.

"You don't understand me. I don't like this boring drudgery. You and Dad have lived in the countryside all your lives. Does that mean I have to live that way too? No. I will leave whether you agree or not!" I shouted at my mother.

"You say that I don't understand you, but can you understand a mother's heart? If you continue with your education, I have no objections. We used our influence and found a job for you, a stable and decent job. Others envied you but instead of appreciating it you quit after only a few months. I don't even know how to explain it to others. Why are you so determined to go away to work? Do you think it's easy to find employment? And you choose Shenzhen – a place so far away from your home. If you went somewhere closer by, it would be easy to get home if you didn't find a job. If you go to Shenzhen and don't find a job or have some accident, you cannot get home without money!"

Mom had never been so agitated. Seeing her strained and anxious face, I felt bad. Although my resolve faltered a little, my stubborn temperament held me to my decision…. I must get away. I couldn't live this life for one more day.

"I'm going off to work, not to fight in the army, so I'm not going to have any accidents. Besides, I'll go mad if I carry on with this life. I'm not interested in playing with naughty children. Mom, I will take care of myself, find a good job, and earn money there, and then come back and look after you. You surely want your son to get ahead in the world, don't you?"

Blue veins standing out on her temples, my mother was so angry that she could hardly speak. She gave a deep sigh and said, "You're determined to go and I cannot stop you. I don't need you to look after your dad and me, and I don't need you to get ahead; I only want you to live a good life. Wait another two days, and Mom will make your favorite dumplings."

With these words, she turned round and walked away. I saw her lift a hand and wipe her eyes. I felt bad, but told myself: Mom, your son will succeed!

During the next two days, Mom helped me pack my bags, while giving me all sorts of "useful" advice. I didn't pay much attention to her words. I was going off to work; there was no need for all this fuss. She contacted an acquaintance to help me find a job. I was touched. Although she didn't want me to leave home, she finally gave in, and now she was arranging matters for me. I didn't think it would be necessary to contact her friend, but to set her mind at ease I promised to contact that person as soon as I got to Shenzhen.

It's Talent Market, Not Labor Market

So I bid farewell to my parents and the town where I had lived for 18 years, and took my bags with me to my dream city – Shenzhen. When I arrived, everything looked so new. I swore passionately to myself that, succeed or fail, I would never go back.

Unfortunately, the good times did not last long. In a few days, half of the 1,000 yuan I had brought with me was gone. I spent the money on renting a home and buying some daily necessities. It went so quickly that I would soon use up all of my money. If I carried on without any specific goal, I would have no money left for food within a month. I must find a job as soon as possible.

To comfort my mother I contacted her acquaintance, who helped me find a job in a company in downtown Shenzhen. The company's business was in mobile phones, and I became a porter in the delivery department.

At first, I did not know what was important when handling mobile phones, nor how to organize and stack them. But I learnt from more experienced colleagues over the next few days, and soon understood the process, and the company decided to let me handle a delivery by myself.

I was nervous. And on that day something happened, which sounded an alarm for me and made me decide to make changes. In fact, I went on to encounter such experiences in my later work, and I know now that they are common occurrences; but at the time I was young and impetuous, and I paid the price.

This was my first independent delivery, and there were a large number of mobile phones to be handled. I had to offload them from a truck and stack them in the customer's warehouse, all by myself. Since it was my first independent job, I wanted to make a good start and I worked very hard.

Tired as I was, I managed to work on, applying myself to the job. But the client was ill-natured, and kept shouting at me, "Sort them properly! You! Get them in!"

For a time I managed to keep my temper, telling myself not to get angry because this was my first job and I must complete it successfully on my own. So I said to the client, "Please wait just a little. I will soon have them in. I'm off-loading them right this minute." But he seemed to pay no attention to me, and kept urging me on. After a while he began to get on my nerves, and I whispered to myself, "Oh just have a bit of patience."

But even such a trivial comment outraged him. He burst into a storm of abuse, "Who do you think you are? A porter! A nobody like you can be so arrogant! You don't want this job? I'll get your boss to fire you!"

All I could do was smile wryly to myself. How come the customer was so unreasonable? Just take it as bad luck, I thought. You can't pick a fight with him. So I carried on with my work. I sweated my way to the end of the job, and made my way back to the company. But before I even had time to tell my colleagues what had happened, I was told that the manager wanted to see me.

I knocked on his door and saw him standing with his back to me, his hands clasped behind his back. Instead of turning round, he spoke quickly and angrily, "Do you know what's the most important thing in our service industry? You quarreled with our customer today! That's completely unacceptable! Who are our customers? They are God, that's who! Do you understand that? I don't want to hear your excuses. This month, your bonus will be cut by 50 yuan."

"For what?"

"Because you're a porter! You're there to serve other people!"

I felt angry. The more I thought about it, the angrier I became. I was angered at being scolded like a child. For all the abuse I had put up with from the customer, I had finished the job in hand. And now I was being criticized instead of rewarded. Did I deserve that? Why was I being treated like that? Porters are human beings too. If a porter in Shenzhen had to put up with this kind of humiliation, I would find something else.

At eight o'clock in the morning the following weekend, I got to the human resources market half an hour earlier. But in front of the big hall, there were already long queues and huge crowds of people. I had second thoughts. But thinking again of that unreasonable client and the way the manager had spoken to me, I decided to take my place in the queue. I waited for four hours before I even got in.

Once I got into the hall, I was even more astonished. There were tens of thousands of people crowded into this hall of no more than 6,000 sq m! I had no idea where to go, and the crowds pushed me from left to right. I felt tiny in this mass of people, like an ant trying to find food in the big city of Shenzhen.

On other resumes, I could see entries like university graduate, two years of work experience, and various certificates. Looking at the two thin sheets of my resume, I blushed with shame: Who am I? No diploma, no experience, and not even any strength. If it hadn't been for my mother's contact, I wouldn't even have had the opportunity to be reprimanded! What a come-down. Before coming here, I thought there were lots of jobs in Shenzhen and I could easily support myself and earn plenty of money. But now I'm at a loss what to do.

When I handed in my application form, my face began to burn with embarrassment. Seeing others' skepticism, I was so ashamed that I just wanted to find a hole in the ground and hide. One man even sneered at me, "Hey! Are you in the right place? This isn't a labor market, you know."

In low spirits, I walked to the bus station and got on the first bus that stopped. I didn't even check whether it was the right bus. The scene from the human resources market, and that man's words, came back to me again and again. I was upset and did not know what to do next. Lost in my thoughts, I didn't come back to reality until the conductor called me. It was the terminal. Looking at the busy conductor in her fifties, it seemed that everyone else in this city was working their way toward a right future!

Three Kinds of Life

When I got back to my dormitory, it was getting dark. I saw playing cards and beer cans on the table; they held little attraction for me. Was this to be my life? Go to work, drink beer, play cards, read boring magazines…. Time would pass like this day after day. Should I waste my youth away like this? Lead such an aimless life? Then when I got old and couldn't carry cases of mobile phones, what would become of me? How could I even survive and live in this city, far less establish myself and prosper here?

As I was thinking, my roommate Liu came back. In his twenties, he was handsome and smart. At the age of 16, he had enrolled into Nanjing University of Aeronautics and Astronautics. After graduation, he had arrived in the company six days later than me. Of similar age and both coming from Hubei, we had a good relationship.

He sighed at the sight of my bleak face, and said, "There's something I've wanted to tell you for a while, but I didn't really know you at the time. Now you're so down, and I feel I must speak out. Pardon me if I seem blunt.

"Those who have high aims but no real ability will quickly change jobs. But they have no diploma or work experience, and they'll find their wages dropping and their lifestyle deteriorating. Eventually they'll choose to leave and go back to the villages they came from.

"Those who are content with things as they are will carry on here, until they're no longer fit for work. Then they too will leave the city and go back to their villages.

"Those who have dreams and long-term plans will keep learning. Through their own efforts, they will win themselves a bright future.

"In three years from now, Shenzhen will be full of university graduates. You won't have any edge in competition. If you don't start to change things, maybe even tomorrow, you will find that university graduates joining the company later than you will be promoted ahead of you. To be cast aside by the city, or to succeed in becoming an office worker – you have a choice to make!"

Cast aside? Cast aside! Would I be cast aside by the city? What a dreadful prospect! The three kinds of people he talked about looked like a junction of three roads of life. I had to make a choice. I came to the city with a smile – would I trudge home in tears? No, I must be a strong person, a winner! I must keep learning!

Kept Awake by the Gap between Managers and Me

That night I lay awake, thinking again and again about the manager who had laughed at me at the human resources market. From then on, Liu's words were constantly in my ears. But I had only just found work, and had already spent almost all the money I had brought from home; where could I find money for further study? I was troubled by this problem and so I put it aside.

Time flew past. A month later, it was time to collect my wages. That day, I went to the bank with excitement, thinking that I would have enough money to have a good meal. All my money was gone, and I had been living off instant noodles for the past few days; even so, I still owed dozens of yuan to my colleagues. But now I could breathe a sigh of relief.

I stood in a queue, singing to myself. But when I checked my account, I was stunned: only a little more than 500 yuan! Was that all my income for a whole month? Payment for all my hard work from morning to night? Five hundred yuan for a month? I could hardly believe it. How could I live in Shenzhen on 500 yuan a month? Even if I bought nothing else, food alone would cost 400-500 yuan. How could I pay to study at an evening school with so little money? It wasn't even possible to eat half-decent food! I could only hope that next month I would earn more. Then I would save some money for further study later....

Life went on uneventfully. One day, my manager asked me to go to his office and help him deal with a work problem.

That day the company had sent out a truck-load of mobile phones, but the client had not received his delivery by the end of the working day. Two fixed-line telephones and the manager's mobile phone rang constantly, and he kept fielding calls. I could only sit and wait, helpless. Sometimes, the manager was answering three calls at once. I could see that he remained calm and sober-minded while taking the phone calls and dealing with the incident.

Within half an hour, he answered nearly 90 calls. And over this period, he successfully sorted the matter out. He calmed the angry client; he found out who should be accountable; mobile phones were delivered to the client as quickly as possible. The company suffered no damage either to its revenues or to its image.

Witnessing the manager so quick to settle the problem and limit any losses, I was conscious of the gap between him and me. When might I stand on the same level as him? How could I develop such competence?

A month earlier, I had insisted on leaving home in spite of my parents' opposition. If I kept on living like this and then was cast aside by the city, how could I face my parents? I had told myself that I would not go home if I did not succeed. I really needed to study and further my career.

Working and Studying

Since I did not have much money, I had to follow a training class, instead of attending a school. But after a while, I found out that my educational level was not good enough, making me slow to learn and preventing me from achieving the desired results. I faced the prospect of being thrown out before I could catch up. With such a weak knowledge base, I had a lot to learn. I needed to follow some structured course of schoolwork.

But with such a low income, I could not work and study at the same time. I had put aside less than 1,000 yuan after working for six months. How could I live? Where could I get money to pay tuition fees? How could I study properly?

What I could do was to turn to my mother for help. I asked for three days' leave and went home. I talked it over with Mom, she agreed to support me though she was concerned that a life of both work and study would prove too hard.

When I returned to the company, I was promoted to a position of warehouse keeper. I was no longer a porter, and this left me with more money, and enough energy to study.

The money problem had been settled, but a more complicated problem arose. I had been away from school for more than six months, and I found it difficult to master what I was learning; I therefore had difficulty in reviewing lessons. Fortunately I could ask Liu for help when he was in the dormitory.

After a period of reflection, I came to the conclusion that I was as able as a high school graduate. So in 2003 I decided to study at the evening school of Shenzhen University, majoring in financial management.

This life of combined study and work was harder than I had expected. Usually, I got off duty after 10 o'clock in the evening; after doing some bits and pieces it was past 11. I had to be at work by 8 the next morning. I was tired after work and had almost no time to study. At the company, I did not have any free time, and was putting in more than 10 hours a day. After work all I wanted to do was sleep, and I was so tired that I didn't even want to chat, far less study.

A boss wants to turn a profit, not make time for his employees to study, which is a problem. If you don't do well at work you're going to get fired; that's the reality. Sometimes, I was getting ready to attend a class when suddenly the company would ask me to work overtime. I couldn't say no. If I wanted to study, I could only use my lunch break, just one or two hours. I needed to avoid attracting the boss's attention; if he saw me studying he would pay extra attention to my work, and try to find some pretext for finding fault with me.

Before I started evening school, I occasionally went out with friends or colleagues. But after I started school, there were no more opportunities for leisure. First, because I didn't have the time, and second, because I didn't have the money. I had borrowed money from home to pay for my studies – I couldn't fritter that money away.

Off and on, I had more than three years of schooling at Shenzhen University, and completed almost all the required courses, with the exception of English, which was my biggest problem. Although I had studied it before starting evening school, I had almost forgotten what I had learned. I had a weak base and had not used it for a long time. Fortunately, the evening school allowed me to take exams in other courses first and postpone the English exam.

English posed a great challenge to my life of work and study. I struggled to remember a few words, but later could not recognize them when seeing them again. If I could not solve this problem, I would never get my degree. Then I would have to ask my old parents for even more money. So I called home and explained my problem. Mom said little, only asking me to go home.

Quitting the Job to Pursue My Education

As soon as I got home, Mom burst into tears and said that I would not have come home if I didn't need her help. In all these years, for the sake of my studies, I had never gone back home to spend Spring Festival with my family.

Although my mother agreed to support me, she could not understand why I had quit the position of department manager that I had only just been promoted to, in order to resume my schooling.

I told her that I had been working there for four years and was reluctant to quit. But it had taken me more than four years to become a department manager, while a university graduate could achieve the same in little more than a year.

I told her Liu's story. He had a university diploma and a good job with generous wages and benefits, but he had left it to spend six months studying at home, and then gone on to become a postgraduate student at Wuhan University, majoring in mobile telecommunications. How difficult must it be to take postgraduate entrance exams for another major? He had already earned a bachelor's degree, but still he aspired to a master's degree. What about me? I only had a certificate of secondary education. A person without a university diploma would never get on in the world.

Mom was touched by the sight of me accompanied by my English books and a dictionary even at home. To create a quiet environment for me to study, she tidied up a room in my grandpa's house. Seeing how much she cared about me, I felt sorry for the graceless way I had spoken to her years before. It's true that parents devote all their love to their children.

After resting for a couple of weeks at home, I returned to Shenzhen to prepare for the English exam. After the exam, I will be able to look for a better job, and lighten the burden on my family.

Looking forward, I'm confident that I will succeed. I will keep studying. And if I have the chance, I will go on to take postgraduate entrance exams in the future.

My Grandpa

Narrator: Chen Fei, male, 20, from Jidian Village in Xiaochang County, Hubei Province
Job of grandpa: waste collector
Work place of grandpa: Wuhan, Hubei Province

My grandpa was a farmer; he spent almost his whole life in the fields. He kept his mother alive with his own efforts. Later he established a family of his own through the toil of his two hands.

My father was his first child, then came my uncles and my aunt. Life was not easy for a family of 6 people. As they grew up, education became a problem. My grandpa didn't want his children to miss out on the opportunity of schooling. Even in his spare time he would work for others to support his children's tuition.

During the "cultural revolution" (1966-1976), my dad dropped out of school. Like some of his peers, he wanted to build a career for himself, but this dream was never to be realized. At my grandpa's suggestion he learned carpentry; this could be counted on as a skill to support the family.

My uncle was unfortunate. He was born with mental disorder, and didn't receive a full education. From my grandpa, I heard the story that one busy harvesting autumn, he himself was working away from home and no one was taking care of the family farmland. My grandma was worried, as others were out working their fields. My uncle sneaked out in an attempt to help the family, but he suddenly passed out in the field. My grandma waited at home till dusk and there was still no sign of my uncle. She asked the villagers for help. But by midnight he still had not been found.

The next morning, a cowherd found my uncle on a ridge of the field. After emergency treatment, he regained consciousness. Fortunately it was not too cold, otherwise my uncle would have died.

After 1949, ideas of equality between men and women were reinforced. But in the village, people continued to attach more importance to men than to women. My grandpa's family was not well-off, so my aunt suffered limits on her freedom. She was diligent and hardworking in her studies, and always ranked first in the class. But limited by family poverty and her parent's ideas of what was appropriate, she only finished primary school. Then she bid a tearful farewell to school life.

My youngest uncle was a very good student. He was top of his class from primary school to high school. He didn't let the family down. Being the youngest, he received more love from the parents and care from his brothers, because he was the hope of the family.

In due course my father reached the age to marry. Many of his peers settled down, but my father had to work to support the family. My grandpa understood this. He himself worked even harder. That autumn he sold all the year's harvest and put aside some money – just enough to allow my father to get married.

My mother suffered ill-health after I was born. She didn't have much breast milk to feed me. We couldn't afford expensive milk powder. My father could only buy cheap product, and in my first days I did not enjoy good health.

Then one day my grandpa discovered a "treasure." While fetching water he suddenly realized that the pond was full of fish. He called my father and they opened the lock. The next morning the water had drained away, and the mud of the empty pond was strewn with fish. My father and grandpa filled two buckets. My grandma cooked a fish soup, and my dad took it carefully up to my mom. My mother's health improved after eating the soup. She produced more breast milk and my health improved too.

When I was two, my second uncle and my aunt both got married. At first others were conscious of my second uncle's mental disorder, and no one would marry him. Fortunately he was a diligent man, and a good worker. He also took good care of his health. He succeeded in attracting a girl, and she married him. My aunt was happy with a simple life, and she was also very beautiful. She chose a good man, and my grandpa was happy to see how things had turned out.

My grandpa's final effort was for his youngest son. When my third uncle was a student, my grandpa would often visit him at school and take him food that he liked. But one day in class my uncle suddenly fainted. Grandpa took him to the county hospital, and after examination he was told that my uncle had chronic hepatitis. On the doctor's advice, grandpa procured some medicine and went home with my uncle. That night he didn't sleep a wink, but spent the hours smoking. The doctor had told him that there was no effective cure for my uncle's illness. The best treatment would be a combination of Western medicine and traditional Chinese medicine. There were many foods that he could no longer eat. But my uncle's health deteriorated.

The cure was a long drawn-out affair. My uncle's health grew steadily poorer, and my grandpa grew increasingly worried. He needed to find a solution. But the family could not afford the high medical costs involved. A few *mu* of farmland could not support the family's needs.

Under this pressure, and knowing there were no prospects of supporting the family from the land, my grandpa, who came from generations of farmers, went off to work as a migrant. He had to find a solution elsewhere.

10 Years to Cure My Uncle's Disease

My grandpa had little education. He knew nothing other than working the fields. His plan was to search for work in the cities. At that time going to work in the cities was a subject of lively debate. Tales abounded of migrant workers who were making a fortune in the cities.

My grandpa had no notions of making his fortune. His only thought was to save some money for his children and grandchildren, and to cure my third uncle's illness. He chose to go to Wuhan, opened the gateway, and left the mountains.

On his first day he wandered around, familiarizing himself with the streets of the city. That evening he found lodgings in a simple house, with one table and several beds, five or six people living together. The room was small and dark, but the rent was cheap. Migrant workers would save money whenever they could.

Grandpa got up early the next morning. Armed with a pair of baskets, he began his job – collecting refuse. He sold what he collected to a recycling center, and was paid 10 yuan. This was the first sum of money he earned in Wuhan.

After a month, grandpa mailed the money he had earned to the family for medical expenses for my uncle. With the treatment, my uncle's illness was contained.

My third uncle is a man who loves to study. Even ill at home he continued his studies. He refused to quit. He wanted to get out of the mountains through his own efforts. The senior high school enrollment exam approached, and he entered it with confidence. But he failed the exam.

In the face of this news, grandpa was not as disappointed as my uncle had expected. Grandpa knew hepatitis had a serious impact on a child. He advised my uncle to try again the following year. But uncle gave it up. He didn't want to go to school, because many people steered clear of any child with hepatitis. He couldn't stand this reaction any longer. More importantly, he didn't want to increase the burden on grandpa. At the age of 18, he wanted to leave school and start his career. Grandpa had no alternatives to offer. How could he not feel the pain of seeing his child reduced to this? He had to accept the inevitable.

Grandpa was still collecting refuse, selling it, and mailing the money back home. He still kept up his hopes of seeing my uncle cured. Through his toil, he managed to support my uncle's medical expenses. And under the family's care, my uncle's illness went into remission.

By 1990 my uncle was 20 years old. He had suffered no relapses. He decided to go to the south. Seeing his passion, grandpa agreed. Laden down with bags, my uncle took the train.

But the lack of a diploma made his life difficult. Even more painful to him were the rejections he experienced from employers when they saw he had suffered from hepatitis. He went to many a factory interview, but found nothing. He took to smoking as a way to endure his disappointment. Finally he had a stroke of luck when a friend helped him find a job in a factory. But the salary was low, and with his new-found addiction to smoking, he could barely pay his way.

Over the course of more than five years as a migrant worker, my uncle was too busy to take care of himself properly. His health was not stable, neither did he manage to save much money. Finally, he decided to go back home. He found himself the only male laborer in the family, and took on all the manual work. But he made no complaint.

Then one day he fell ill again. Grandpa, who was still in Wuhan, returned home immediately. He knew my uncle's treatment could not be delayed, otherwise the worst might happen. With all his savings he took uncle to the best hospital in the province. A senior doctor patiently gave the benefit of all his experience to my grandpa and my uncle. He wrote out a prescription, and told my grandpa if my uncle followed this treatment for two years his hepatitis would be cured. By that time my uncle was 28 years old, and still unmarried. Few villagers wanted to associate with him for fear that they too would be infected. Some of his peers already had children, but to him the chances were that his children would inherit his hepatitis, so marriage was a problem and he could only stay at home and take his medicines.

My grandpa was still a refuse collector, but some days he earned little. More and more people were going to the city and taking up this business, and so there was more competition. The pressure was on to get up early and work fast, so my grandpa had to get up earlier than before.

Summer Vacation Spent with My Grandpa

It was the summer vacation of my first grade in primary school. My mom took me to Wuhan to see my grandpa. I stayed on with grandpa when my mom went back home, and I spent my vacation with him.

I followed my grandpa's cart, when there was nothing on board grandpa would invite me to sit on the cart and pull it along.

Sometimes after everything had been sold, grandpa would take me to a cheap restaurant and buy me a bottle of soda. He had a beer, and we drank and ate together. After a while we made our way home. The summer in Wuhan was scorching; it was only in the evening after a day's hard work that my grandpa and I could enjoy the freshness of the night.

When the new semester approached, grandpa took me home. He also brought medicines for my uncle.

My grandpa's efforts finally paid off. After two years of treatment, my uncle's hepatitis was completely cured. All the family was delighted. After 10 years of toil as a migrant worker, grandpa had cured the disease through his hard work and frugality.

Grandma advised him not to go off to work anymore, but he wouldn't listen. Although work in the city was hard going, he could earn better money. He picked up his bags once more and headed off. Two years later he came home again, and the money he brought was enough for my third uncle to get married.

A Child Left at Home

Soon after my third uncle got married, his son was born. Grandpa was very pleased to have one more grandson.

Now a father, my uncle began to feel the pressure of supporting his family. He could not think only of himself; he had a wife, a child and two parents to care for.

He leased a pond in the village, and planted seeds all around it to feed the fish. The couple worked hard for two years, hoping to make their fortune. But they lacked experience, and their fish were of poor quality. They were also hit by flood that allowed many of their fish to escape. They lost money. Finally the couple decided to give up fish farming, and go off to work as migrant workers. That October they headed south, leaving the child with my grandpa.

My grandpa was opposed to the idea, but he could not stop them. They left just before Spring Festival. How long till they would be back? Three years, four, or five? Uncle couldn't tell grandpa. He said only that they would return once they had earned the money to build a house. Looking at his cute grandson, grandpa was filled with confusion, because in his heart he knew that accepting this child meant taking on a big responsibility. He loved the boy, but he worried whether he would be able to provide him with a proper education.

When the grandson was three years old, grandpa decided to send him to a nearby village kindergarten, and he himself go back to work in the city again.

Before he left he told his wife repeatedly to take care of the grandson, and protect him from cold and hunger. Grandma carried a heavy burden. She had to take care of the fields, and she had to take care of the grandson. She got up early every day to make breakfast, then sent the child to kindergarten. After school she would bring him back home.

Day after day she took care of him, as a full-time nanny.

Two years later, my uncle came back in the spring. He was very happy to come home to see his son. But the boy did not recognize him, and wouldn't call him dad. Uncle tried to tempt his son with treats brought back from the south to get closer to the child.

He checked how well the boy had studied. But his son knew nothing. He couldn't even do simple arithmetic. Uncle was worried and angry. He complained of grandma's failing to discipline the child. Grandma said nothing in response, and simply accepted the blame.

At that time, village kindergartens were run by village teachers, who didn't have any teaching qualifications. They taught in order to feed their own families. They hadn't gone through any formal training and therefore they could teach the students little. When he realized this, uncle stopped blaming grandma. He knew that it was critical for a child to learn when he was four or five years old, so after thinking things over carefully, he decided to take the boy south to get an education. He took grandma along as well.

Grandpa's Mental Disorder

Grandpa learned of their plan the day before they left. He wanted grandma and the child to stay, but he couldn't come up with any good argument. So he told himself: as long as it is best for them and good for the boy's future, it is the right thing to do. He left before they did, and went back to his work as a refuse collector.

Grandpa rarely came back to the village after they left. Spring Festival was a lonely time for him. One night, he suddenly leaped from his bed in a fit of madness, and rushed out of the house naked. He was making such a racket that the neighbors were wakened. They came out and found grandpa kneeling in the hay in the cowshed. Some young men tried to pick him up and he suddenly ran away. No one could see him in the dark. The village head led the others in a search for him, and they finally found him huddled up by the river. They put some clothes on him and got him back to bed.

Hearing this, uncle immediately hurried back with grandma. They took grandpa to a mental hospital. The doctor said it was a mental disorder, but grandpa had never showed any symptoms before. Possibly it was some kind of recessive hereditary disease. Many external factors might be the cause of the attack. The doctor also said that it could be caused by psychological trauma or depression. The doctor was not sure whether it would happen again in the future. His family needed to care for grandpa and protect him from any psychological strain. Uncle decided to leave grandma with grandpa to care for him.

Before he left, uncle bought more than 1,000 yuan of medicines. Under grandma's care, grandpa's health and mood improved.

"I didn't know what I was doing when I ran out in the night," Grandpa recalled. "I finally jumped into the river several miles from the village. I don't know why. The water was freezing in winter, and the cold brought me back to my senses. Otherwise I might have died in the river."

Life in a Corner of the City .

In March, grandpa packed his bag to go back to work in the city. Grandma wanted him to stay at home, but he wouldn't listen. She was afraid that if grandpa took ill again in the city it would be a major problem. So she decided to go with him. By then he was suffering from advanced prostate disease. He had to take pills for this, and also for the mental disorder. These medicines represented a big outlay. None of his children were well-off. Already they were struggling to maintain their independence, and now grandpa was suffering from this new ailment. The reason he worked so hard as a migrant worker was that he wanted to cure his illness. As he said with a sigh, "Poor people are afraid of falling ill."

Grandpa and grandma went to Wuhan. They still lived in an obscure corner of this modern metropolis, in a simple dwelling. For a migrant worker it would be enough to have a place to sleep and to shelter from the rain. Grandpa didn't ask for more.

Grandma worried that my uncle's child was not being cared for properly in the south. So they brought him back and found a school for him. There was a new policy that students from villages no longer had to pay additional tuition fees at schools in the cities. The school was not far, but she was worried he might get lost on the way. For the first few days they accompanied him to school and taught him the way. Later, he didn't need his grandparents to escort him.

One winter afternoon I went to visit. The house was dark and dim, and grandma was sorting refuse in the corner. Everything that could be sold would be saved, the rest would be discarded. Seeing me, grandma tried to hurry her work and clear it all up. "Take your time," I said.

"Have you eaten?" she asked and got up to make some supper for me. I told her I had already eaten at school. She said to me, "I need to do something to keep myself busy. It's a kind of habit. I collect refuse and keep some for your grandpa to sell. It doesn't amount to much, but every little helps."

Grandpa came back at dusk. He was very happy to see me. He asked about my school life, and how my studies were going.

The following day, he went to the market and bought pork ribs for grandma to cook. Then he went out to work again. I had nothing to do after eating, so I took my cousin through his homework. Grandma set a fire in the stove. I asked her why it had gone out, and she answered me, "Coal is expensive in winter; we can't afford to burn it from morning to night. We only use the stove when we're cooking, so I light a fire before I start to make a meal." I thought to myself, "That means that grandma has to light the fire three or four times a day...." But I knew it made sense from a financial point of view. Would I have the patience to do something like that? My grandparents have been through many a difficult time, and it is never easy for them to earn money.

After supper I strolled in the street. I saw other people also lighting their stoves – among them was one old couple. I was shocked. This is the real life of the migrant workers. They live in simple houses, and they do their best to save money for their family. They don't ask for much, and they don't live in the cities out of choice. All they want is a better life for themselves and their children. They live in obscure corners of the cities, and they lead obscure lives.

I was lost in thought. Grandpa and grandma had worked hard for most of their lives, and they still have to work now. Grandpa has to earn money because of his health problems. They are responsible for bringing up my uncle's child. In this metropolis, only through saving money can you have a little extra and satisfy the needs for life.

I told grandpa I would go home the next day. He invited me to stay for a few days longer, but I refused.

There was a train leaving at 4 in the morning. I got up at 3, packed my things and got ready to leave. Grandpa woke up, gave me 20 yuan, and said it was for my train ticket. Usually I was happy enough to take even 100 yuan. But on this occasion I felt that 20 was too much. Grandpa finally forced it on me. It was cold and I asked grandpa to go back to bed. I closed the door quietly, hoping I hadn't woken my grandma or my cousin. I walked to the bus station alone, with the money in my hand.

Still a Migrant Worker in My 60s

Narrator: Fu Yunlai, male, 63, from Lüzhai County, Guangxi Zhuang Autonomous Region
Job: construction worker – stevedore – shipment worker – vendor
Work place: Dongguan – Shenzhen – Zhuhai in Guangdong, Nanning – Liuzhou in Guangxi

I am an ordinary farmer. When I was 40 I left my home village for the city and became a migrant worker. Twenty-three years of hard work in the cities have passed since then. I've done countless jobs: fruit vendor, beer bottle collection, construction worker, shipment worker, security guard …. I've worked in almost all fields of manual labor.

At 63, other people have grandsons and enjoy a good family life. But I still have to labor to earn a living. I have no choice. I have a son who also works in the city as a migrant worker and does not earn much money – just enough not to need extra money from us. I'll continue working until the day I am no longer able.

School Life

My time as a student might make good material for a book. Students today would have a hard time writing a book about their life.

They are busy every day, they have to read so many books at such a young age, and take so many exams. Our schoolbag was essentially a sack. At that time, there was no pressure to study hard; it didn't make much difference whether you studied well or badly.

We studied and worked at the same time. We had five days of classes and two days of voluntary labor. Every class had a field in which the students could plant sugar cane, vegetables, sweat potatoes, and taro. Our task was to cultivate the land, and when the crops were harvested, we would take the produce to market. The money earned would be for class expenditure, and we could go out and have a bit of fun. Thinking back, our life as students was good – we didn't have to work too hard and we had plenty of fun.

Our teacher was very strict, though. He taught us to write, and if we wrote a single word wrong, we would have to rewrite it 1,000 times! The boys often misbehaved, and those who broke the class rules, like me, were often punished and made to stand at the back of the classroom. By the time the punishment was over, the class was also over. It was no big problem for me, as I didn't want to study anyway. How boring I thought it was! I didn't get good grades. My parents didn't insist on the importance of learning, as long as I could write my name and knew some basic arithmetic. They were farmers all their lives, with very little education of their own, and they couldn't help me.

My classmates went on to senior high school after junior high. Some of them even went to college after the "cultural revolution" came to an end. They now live good lives – some are government officials, some are commanding officers in the army, some are business leaders with salaries of hundreds of thousands. If I worked hard for a lifetime and didn't eat or drink, I wouldn't earn that much. When I was young I was naughty and mocked them because they studied hard. Now I realize I was foolish. "A youth spent in idleness, an old age spent in need" – I didn't know the meaning of that as a child. Now I understand, but too late.

There were many children in the village who left school after junior high. At that time importance was attached to productive work, not to science and learning. And I was no diligent student. I wanted to have fun and earn money. I was young, and I went to work in the fields.

Going to the City in Search of Opportunity

Our family was relatively big, and had little land. We could only harvest 350 to 400 kg of crops, but once the cost of fertilizer and tool hire was deducted, we could only earn 300 to 400 yuan. After a year of hard work, the whole family would earn only some 1,000 yuan. This money was supposed to keep a dozen people. We were poverty-stricken. Five years of farming were like this, and 10 years were the same. When I was 40, people from the village began to go to cities to work. They said they could earn 100 yuan a month working in cities. I made up my mind to join them.

What was it like in the cities? What could I do? Could I survive? Were the city people good....? Time goes by, and these doubts have still not been solved. More than 20 years have passed, and I've been to Dongguan, Shenzhen and Zhuhai in Guangdong, Nanning and Liuzhou in Guangxi, and also the surrounding counties. I've been in small business, worked as a construction laborer, as a shipyard worker. All these jobs are arduous, but I have no choice because I have neither money nor skills. I also don't have ideas of my own; I can only work for others.

After years of work I had a little money saved. In 1990 I spent

900 yuan and bought a three wheeled cycle. It was more convenient for me to carry goods or sell products. At first I collected beer bottles. I rode my three-wheeler up lanes and down streets, banging an old piece of iron and shouting, "Beer bottles and cardboard boxes!" Sometimes I had to knock on every door to get anything. At that time a beer bottle was worth 25 cents, and I took 5 cents for myself. If I was lucky I might get one or two *Moutai* bottles – one of them would sell for several yuan. But only a few people could afford *Moutai*. This job needed a loud voice and perseverance. Not only did I have to spend the whole day riding around and shouting, but the income was unstable. We usually collected small quantities of bottles from individual households, from a few dozens to around a hundred. Restaurants sold them in large quantity, but our cart was small, so sometimes we couldn't take them all. We were doing well if we could earn more than 10 yuan a day. Sometimes people thought you were charging too much and raised the price, from 25 to 26 cents. Housewives were difficult to deal with. We would often bargain for ages over a question of 1 or 2 cents, or else they wouldn't sell their bottles to me because other people would collect them.

As time passed, fewer and fewer people were collecting beer bottles. It was tiring work and you didn't earn much. What else could I do? I had a three-wheeler – there must be other alternatives. I could sell things, or be a vegetable vendor. I decided to spend some money buying vegetables from the suburb and selling them at the market in town. There would be some profit, without too much outlay, so the risk was small.

I had to get up early to buy the vegetables, around 1 or 2 o'clock in the morning. I would choose my vegetables, bargain, take them back to the city, and get there just in time to sell them. I had to sell what I bought the same day. The vegetables wouldn't keep for a second day. The more I was left with, the more I would lose. Fruit was a better business – the produce would stay fresh for longer. But the business of selling fruits and vegetables always created the problem of disposing of them quickly. As long as we could sell them for something, we had a little money.

Trying to Get Delayed Salaries

The people from my village work in different jobs, but most of them work on construction sites. The job is dirty and tiring, and poorly paid. How many city people would want to do it? The advantage in hiring us is that we are able to endure hardship – we are not afraid of dirt and weariness. We would work as a group together when a job started, then when it finished we would make our way to the next job. We would eat simple pre-cooked food which only cost a few yuan; we would live in a temporary shelter of bricks and wood. As long as we had food, a place to sleep, and a small wage, it was sufficient for a migrant worker's need.

Urban construction needs migrant workers. If you are competent at the task and can do it well, you are guaranteed a living. You will follow the construction contractor to various sites. Contractors are not always pleasant people, when they need you they will be polite to you, but when there are no jobs they will not even give you a second glance. Frankly I don't care to argue about this. As long as I have a job, a meal, and my wage, other things are of no importance. The worst that can happen is that after finishing a hard job the contractor doesn't pay you. What do you do then – accept it? Leave with nothing?

In 2004, together with some townsfolk, I worked for a construction contractor. We worked for six months to build a road in Liuzhou. The job was done, the construction finished, but the contractor did a runner! He went off with the salaries of more than 100 migrant workers. Three years passed and I still hadn't got my money. Our families all had elderly relatives and children; our children had to go to school; I had already borrowed money from relatives and friends. Still they wouldn't pay us – who could we turn to? The head of the construction company was evasive, and there came a time when we couldn't even track them down! Altogether, it came to more than 400,000 yuan of salary. We hadn't been paid a penny for our hard work, and eventually they said they wouldn't pay us the whole sum. There was to be a 25% deduction. We weren't a department store. A man's salary can't be discounted. This was money that we had earned through honest labor! Were they going to offer a discount on their building? The lunar new year was approaching, and we were all hoping to get our money and go home to be with our families. Instead we were stuck here without the means to pay for our children's tuition or our rent. What were we supposed to live off?

We have asked for these delayed salaries again and again. We've held protests. But every time promises were made and nothing has been delivered. I really have no idea what to do. I look at my townsfolk and I look at myself. We look much older than our real age. Our hands are worn by cement, our faces covered in wrinkles. Rarely do we ever wear neat, smart clothes.

But this is my fate, and there is no use complaining. My family has been farmers for generations, and I have no skills. It is impossible for me to be a high official or to get rich. But at least I got out of the village. I've been to many places and seen many things. This is some kind of progress.

I Personally Feel Remote from Urban People

I sometimes worked as a floor tiler. I might be criticized by the hostess if I crossed a room to drink water; she would say that my shoes were dirty and made her house dirty. Sometimes I met nicer people who would tell me that I didn't need to take my shoes off — just walk in the house as you are. That gave me a feeling of warmth — the idea that I could also earn the respect of city people.

City people's attitudes to migrant workers differ. Some look down upon us, some give us a little basic respect. I can say that working in cities is only a little better than working in the fields. But those who still work in the village think we are in the cities as part of the "gold rush." Only we know how difficult it is.

Regrets as a Father

I've worked in cities for more than 20 years. Had I known life would be so difficult I would have studied harder, and my life would have been much better. In my youth I was badly-behaved and didn't want to study. That is something I now regret. My son was like me. He was a good student in primary school. I was proud and thought the family had a great hope. He might go on to college. What I didn't expect was that he would quit his studies after junior high school. He fell in with a bad crowd, and began to cause trouble every day.

My wife and I worked in the city all year long. Our son had only his grandparents to look after him. But they couldn't discipline him. He would argue back when they talked to him. He even took a stick to his grandpa, the wastrel! When I found that out after coming home, I beat him. My mother stopped me, crying. That was the first time I had ever hit my son so hard. This only made matters worse – he would disappear and hardly ever come home. But there wasn't really anything I could do about it. I had to be off earning a living, otherwise who would support the family?

There are so many migrant workers in the cities. If you take so much as a day off work and leave your place open, somebody else will fill it. That "food bowl" you've put so much effort into finding will be lost. Under the pressure of this lifestyle I had to give up on my son. I had thought about taking him with me and letting him study in the city. But the transfer of *hukou* (residence registration) and high tuition fees were both big problems.

I know I was not a good father. I didn't teach him well and I regret it. If I had given him more warmth and care, he might not have gone wrong. Now he has established his own family and matured a bit. I only hope he will teach his child well and help him escape from the fate of the migrant worker. A migrant worker's life is a hard one!

I Choose to Return to School

Narrator: Wu Ting, female, 22, from Jianli County, Hubei Province
Job: packer
Work place: Shenzhen, Guangdong Province

Failure in the College Entrance Exam

Thoughts of July 2003 bring back painful memories for me. When I received my college entrance exam results, I could not help crying. My competitive spirit could hardly tolerate such a failure.

My parents, who were migrant workers in Guangzhou, were told about my exam results over the phone. They didn't criticize me, saying only, "What about trying again next year? A fortune teller foretold that our child would be top of the school." Tears ran down my cheeks and my heart ached at the sound of my parents' kind words of consolation.

My home village didn't have too many able students, and my excellence was widely recognized. Whenever the neighbors talked about me they would say things like, "Ting is such an outstanding girl at school." I felt shy on hearing such words, but happy inside.

I had tried to build up my confidence by winning praise. My

parents worked away from home and were not around for me. So I craved recognition from others. I hoped that when the day came that my parents returned home, they would hear about their outstanding daughter. So failure in the college entrance exam came as a terrible blow to me. My family had very little money, so I decided to go to work in the city.

It was not unusual in our village for a young girl to go to work as migrant worker. If you did not study at school, working in the city seemed the only alternative. I said nothing about my plan to anyone in the family prior to my departure, and went off on my own to look for work in Shenzhen.

A Tricky Interview

I found one of my classmates in junior high and moved in with her. Since I had no skills, nor any college certificate, the idea of finding work easily was an idle dream. I simply hoped to get work in some reasonable place, with accommodation provided.

Helped by my friend's recommendation, I went for an interview in a factory. It was a laboring job, and I thought as long as I was healthy, I should get it. But when I went into the interview room, across the table from me sat three people who looked like supervisors. From the moment I entered the room until I took my seat, they said nothing, but simply looked at me. I was nervous, and had no idea what to say. One of them asked for my name and my educational background. When I answered, I found my throat was dry and my voice was weak. After my simple introduction, they asked me some other questions. I nodded mechanically or shook my head – I couldn't give a sensible answer to anything they asked about me. The only thing I was conscious of was that my mind was a blank and I couldn't even think.

I had expected that a basic introduction would be enough, but I was asked to assemble some product, an activity designed to test the skill of the interviewee. I was surprised by the demanding nature of the interview, which was completely different to what I had been led to expect. But if I was to win a place in the factory I would have to get on with it. The task was to assemble a battery according to the instructions. But my inexperience let me down, and I exceeded the prescribed time. I was told immediately that I failed.

I felt weak, but paused for a short while, then rushed to the supervisors and said, "Please give me another chance – this time I'll finish on time." Perhaps my attitude moved the supervisor, as he agreed. I went back and put the battery together by memory alone. My hands were shaking, and I was in a terrible sweat, but I finished the job with something to spare. I looked at the supervisor anxiously, and heard him say, "Let's sign the contract."

My job was basically the same as the task I had carried out during the interview. During my training period I learned that this was a joint venture. There was a dorm and a canteen, so my problems of eating and accommodation were resolved.

A Fellow Worker's Story

Living in a distant city is lonely, especially when you do not have your family around you. I am a person who is afraid of loneliness. After work I liked to talk with my co-workers, listening to their stories as well as telling my own.

One of my fellow workers was a Chongqing girl called Shasha, whose experiences made me question the wisdom of my choice. She said working as a migrant required either a diploma, physical strength, or manual skills. The toughest and the most arduous option was working as a laborer, and she was a perfect example.

Shasha had previously worked in a privately-owned factory, but because she had no skills, she could only do simple work. There was no overtime for working extra hours. The plant was humid, and the air was full of dust. Wages were often delayed; under pressure the boss would hand out only enough of the overdue payments to keep the workers quiet.

Shasha's mother passed away suddenly, so she quit the job and asked for her unpaid salary. However the factory said there were some procedures to be dealt with and she was delayed. By the time all these procedures were complete, her mother had already been buried for several days. I asked Shasha why she would ever work in such a place. She smiled and said, "Who could have known that the factory would be like this? I was glad enough to find a job to keep me going – we don't have the luxury of making choices."

I told Shasha the story of my time in junior high, and about my failure in the college entrance exam. She showed wisdom beyond her years, pointing out that my parents had offered me the choice of continuing my studies, however hard it would have been for them, and I should have cherished this offer. I was taken aback by her words – had I made a mistake by going out to work as a migrant?

Shasha told me that in her family, her mother had suffered from ill-health for many years, with the result that only her father, a carpenter, was able to work. The family could not support school fees for both herself and her brother. If she had the choice she would stand outside the schoolroom window to listen to classes rather than work in this place. I suddenly felt troubled, and began to question myself. I didn't want to be distracted from my chosen course of action, but when I heard Shasha's words, the strength of my resolve began to crumble.

Embarrassment over a Bottle of Water

Although we were working in an unfamiliar city, we liked to walk around during our leisure time. This metropolis was an expensive place, and we could not afford to spend money on parks and other scenic sites. One time we heard that if you went into the Jinshawan seaside resort through the back gate, you wouldn't have to pay for a ticket. We sneaked in from the back, but as we were not familiar with the road, the guard soon found us and we had to pay for our tickets. Ten yuan may be nothing to others, but we would live on that amount for a whole day.

We walked in the park and saw many people in fashionable clothes. They gave us some odd looks. I know they didn't mean any harm, but I am a sensitive person, and I couldn't cope with this attention, so I suggested we find a quieter spot for our stroll.

After a while, we all felt thirsty. We stopped at a stall and found that a bottle of water that would cost 1 yuan outside was priced at 5 yuan here. We hesitated and heard one of the stallholders whisper to another, "They wouldn't buy it." Although she said it very quietly, we all heard her clearly. I felt embarrassed, and my friends were upset as well. Finally the four of us bought one bottle of water between us. For all that we were thirsty, we only sipped.

It was at times like this that I missed my family and my simple, happy times at school.

Relationship Problems in the Factory

It was hard to make real friends in the factory.

My job was packaging, which didn't require much in the way of skill, as long as you were dexterous. But I had problems with my partner Huang Wan. We were supposed to work together and split the production requirement equally. But Huang would often chat with others while working, and my workload grew heavier. Yet still the production recorded for me was the same as hers. I am not the type of person to argue over minor things, nevertheless I fell out with her.

Huang Wan treated me very well when I first came to the factory. While I was still learning the job, she helped me willingly. When I was sick she asked for leave to care for me. So when she offered to work alongside me, I gladly agreed.

But I soon found out that she was a lazybones, and sometimes left the hard work to me. At first I carried on with my work in silence. Eventually a girl from another group spoke to me about it when Huang wasn't around, "Wu Ting, are you stupid? Why do you let her get away with all this?" I said, "I'm a quick worker. I can help her; it's no big deal." Even so, when Huang came back I said, "Don't keep wandering off – finish your share of the work first." She quickly got angry, "What are you talking about? Are you claiming I don't do my share?" I was lost for words. Why would she take advantage of my good nature in this way? I turned away from her glares, finished my work, and went back to the dorm.

After this, things were chilly between us. There was no joking and smiling like before. Eventually, I quarreled with her when she wandered off during work again. My voice grew loud, and my face went red. But she simply sneered back at me. I was left feeling like a naughty child, as if I was the one at fault. Everybody around was looking at us, and my voice gradually died away and I fell silent. I tried to go back to work. But soon Huang started chatting with someone else, just like before, and I was left with all the work to do. My chest was as tight as a drum, and I had no way to relieve the pressure. My heart quailed.

That afternoon I simply left my work and walked out of the factory. I didn't know what to do; I just felt that there was a millstone weighing me down, but I couldn't talk about it to my parents and start them worrying. I also wanted to call some of my high school friends, but I didn't do that either. I didn't want them to know how unhappy I was. After a whole afternoon's absence I finally returned to the factory.

I expected to be punished, because the regulations made it clear that people who left work for no good reason would have their production figures reduced, and might even be fired. But when I went to check the production figures the following morning, my numbers were the same as Huang Wan's. Seeing this, Huang glowered at me. She challenged the woman who was in charge of the records, but got nothing but a rebuke in return. Later, the new section leader got wind of this. He came up and asked me to go outside with him. I knew I was in for some kind of punishment. As I was to leave, Huang Wan darted a look in my direction but said nothing. My lady in charge stopped me, "Wu Ting, just you stay here. I've been the group leader here." The section leader was angry – he walked away.

Not long after I saw Huang Wan in the office of the supervisor, then my kind group leader and the section leader were called in. I felt a pang of unease, and couldn't focus on my work. I didn't want her to get into trouble on my account, so I went to the supervisor and told him the whole story.

I admitted my mistake, and received a deduction of one day's production as punishment. The supervisor changed the method used to record our production to a system where Huang and I each had our output counted separately. At my request, the supervisor agreed not to punish my group leader.

The matter was closed, and Huang Wan was more distant to me after this. She continued to be lazy and her production was a lot lower than before. She was given the cold shoulder by her own colleagues, and shortly afterward she quit the job.

I was sad to see her go. We were all migrant workers, and she had looked out for me. I was not someone who was good at making friends, and her departure made me feel even lonelier.

A Missed Opportunity

I am often hesitant when faced with choices, and when I finally make up my mind, the opportunity is gone.

When I was at school, I was nicknamed "the bookworm." Naturally the factory library became one of my favorite haunts. Every time I went there I would see people borrowing technical books. I felt great respect for them. Later I came to know that most of them were in the research department. They were specialists in battery design.

One day I saw a bulletin on the office billboard, "The company plans to expand into the automobile industry. A school is to be opened, which will hire professional teachers to train sales staff.

People who are interested can register." This school was enrolling students both internally and externally. Following graduation students could get a position in the company. This was an attractive opportunity. If everything went well I could stay at Shenzhen to study and work. But I noticed that after graduation the employee must work at the company for 5 years. Five years is no trivial period of time. I would have to prepare for the test and I would have to pay several thousand yuan in tuition fees, which was no small sum to my family. I went through a period of turmoil, but my desire to study prevailed.

However, by the time I had made up my mind to apply, the examination deadline had already passed. I felt regret, so much so that I couldn't sleep for days. I had had a hard time finding the resolve to act, and now that I had decided to apply there was no longer time.

Making the Decision to Go Home to Study

While I was still regretting my lost opportunity, my working group was allocated to another workshop where demand for batteries was increasing. This job required longer hours than the flexible packaging, and I often had to handle the batteries. Within a week my hands were covered with ulcers that turned the simplest of daily activities into a trial. I even had difficulty holding my chopsticks.

At that time my mother called me and asked how things were going. Naturally I said everything was fine. I didn't mention the missed exam, let alone the state of my hands.

My skin couldn't tolerate the corrosive battery chemicals, and began to blister. I thought of the old days when my hands used to hold pens, now these hands were becoming rough and ugly. I was heartbroken, and longed to go back to school and study.

I was so mixed up that I didn't dare to tell my parents. I only told them I wanted to change my job. It was my father who raised the subject of my going back to school. I thought about whether or not I should tell my parents how much I really wanted to do it. "How will it work when I haven't made any preparations for anything?" I thought to myself. I had heard that the high school mathematics curriculum had changed – would I be able to keep up? All of this made me hesitate.

Although I wanted to go back to school, there were so many things to be taken into account. I talked it over with a friend who was studying at school. She was full of encouragement. With her support, I felt more confident about my choice. I told my father about my decision, and boarded the train home.

I didn't know whether or not I could catch up with fellow students, but it was worth a try. I didn't want to lose the opportunity again.

Enrolled at University

Getting back into school was no easy matter. Many schools were aware of my working experience, and with the fact that my grades weren't the best, they didn't want to accept me. Through an acquaintance my father found a teacher to support me, and after some effort I was accepted by the county high school.

At first I had difficulty getting to grips with my textbooks once more. I had to ask classmates to help me understand the lessons. Sometimes it took me an hour to solve a problem that the others could do in only half the time. I felt angry with myself, and thought I must be stupid. But when I thought back to the experiences of Shasha and the others, it restored my determination to succeed.

After a while I began to re-adjust to school rhythm. The study habit came back to me. I almost found myself immune to feelings of tiredness. I got calls from friends wanting to encourage me. I was happy to be back.

Although I kept myself optimistic, I was worried that others might feel differently when they heard about my background. So I told myself again and again: "Don't think of others, just study hard – you're no different from any other normal student." Finally at graduation, a classmate told me, "Wu Ting, I've never dared to speak to you about it in person. But I admire you enormously for coming back to school after having gone to work as a migrant." I smiled in reply, "I wasn't so sure about it myself...." "We were curious about you at the time, but the teacher told us not to ask about you, and she asked us to help you." I felt great warmth in my heart. My thoughtful classmates had created a wonderful atmosphere for me to study in.

I remember the day when I received my letter of admission to university. My father took the letter and read it over and over again. It was as if the letter might fly away out of his hands if he didn't read every word carefully. Seeing the smile on his face, I knew the best reason for my return. I hope my family will be proud of me. Although they never voiced it aloud, I am well aware of how much they had dreamed of this.

Neighbors came round to offer their congratulations to my mother. She simply answered, "Ting is a good girl." When I saw the smiles on my parents' faces, it made every ounce of my effort worthwhile.

Now as I look back over my experience, I am no longer the naïve child I once was. I think things through more carefully. At university, I may not be one of the best students, but I will try to achieve the best I can.

Compared to my friends who are still working in the cities, I am a lucky girl.

Postscript

This book is a record of the lives of migrant workers. Western readers might not understand who migrant workers are. The term refers to farmers who leave their fields and strive to make a life for themselves in the cities. Their work takes them to the cities, but their homes are in their villages. They are farmers as well as workers. They account for a large proportion of China's population.

"Migrant workers" first appeared in the 1980s, at the beginning of reform and opening-up. The migrant workers included in this book include the first generation, who have already worked for 20 or 30 years, and the second generation, who were born in the 1980s and even the 1990s. Some still continue their itinerant migrant life, some have become entrepreneurs, and some have gone back to school.

They have worked hard for themselves and their families. The hardship of their lives is so palpable that you can taste it as you read. Their stories might seem insignificant and lack grandeur, but each individual experience is built of small incidents that hold great significance for the workers themselves. This was the sensation that we editors felt as we went through the stories.

Why have we published this book? Because we understand how important a role the migrant workers play in society as a whole. They are inseparably linked with China's development over the last three decades. China's reform and opening-up started in the village, and China's manufacturing industry relies heavily on the migrant workers. Migrant workers have made their contributions to economic growth, to political stability, and to the renewal of the whole system. Their tears and sweat are the price that China has paid for reform and opening-up. The dedication that has produced this contribution needs to be recorded. This is the essential aim of this book.

Also, for a host of reasons, migrant workers lack the ability to write and to publish their own life stories. It is essential to capture in writing what they have gone through. This will provide invaluable material for future generations studying the development of modern China.

I hope that this book will help Western readers develop a better understanding of migrant workers, and thereby bring them to a better understanding of contemporary China and the Chinese. But more importantly, I hope that the lives and the work of these migrant workers will improve, one day to match the hopes they carried with them when they left their homes and villages in pursuit of a dream.

The migrant workers have made an enormous contribution to rapid Chinese urban development. They are likely to be found on every skyscraper. This is a migrant worker on Shenzhen's tallest building.

In southeast China there are many manufacturing companies. Since the 1980s, large numbers of farmers have chosen to leave their homes and work here. Pictured are workers leaving their factories at the end of a shift.

Migrant workers have participated in almost every major construction project, such as building bridges and railways like these.

Migrant workers are the main force in small manufacturing companies. A worker in a workshop in Dongwei Village, Shandong Province.

Suburban people travel to the city in search of work, and advertize their skills.

Two soft toys at the post of a female worker in a Shandong printer company
represent a small token of recognition for her productivity.

Temporary job information board at Feiyunjiang Bridge, Ruian of Zhejiang Province.

Every year after the Spring Festival, the number of migrant workers traveling by rail will peak. Anhui Province's Fuyang Railway Station.

To the Chinese people, the Spring Festival is the highlight of the year, and an opportunity to get back to the family. Many migrant workers only travel home once a year. Migrant workers waiting to get into the bus station in Haikou in Hainan Province.

During Spring Festival season, railways, highways, water and air routes are all packed. Some choose to ride home on motorcycles. At noon on January 30, 2011, hundreds rest at a service center in Wuzhou, Guangxi. From January 19 to 30, about 300,000 migrant workers motorcycled home in Guangxi from Guangdong right before the Spring Festival on February 3.

In recent years local governments have arranged professional training programs for migrant workers to give them additional skills. An electrician training migrant workers to install electric equipment.

A new day begins at a construction site in Beijing.

Migrant workers celebrating a festival in Shandong Province.

The dorm, now a ballet stage.

Many migrant couples leave their children behind. Their upbringing and education are a source of concern. Children of Hope Primary School at Shiba Town, Anhui Province, sending letters to their parents.

Some children follow their parents to the cities. They either go to public schools, or to schools opened especially for them. These are students after class in such a school.

The younger generation of migrant workers adopts a more urban lifestyle and dresses more fashionably. Young migrant workers leaving Chongqing and heading back to work in Guangdong and Zhejiang after Lantern Festival of 2010.

In 2009, "Chinese workers" were named "Person of the Year" by *Time* magazine. *Time* commented that Chinese workers had made a huge contribution to China's economic growth and taken a leading role in global economic recovery. Migrant workers are the major force in China's industry.